The Bread Machine Baker

Elizabeth M. Harbison

Barnes & Noble Books
New York

ABOUT THE AUTHOR

ELIZABETH M. HARBISON studied cooking both in the U.S. and Europe and has worked as a private chef in the Washington, D.C. area over the past six years. Her interest in bread machines began on Mother's Day 1991, when she received one as a gift. Since that time she has invented, collected, traded, and tested hundreds of bread machine recipes, often serving them to her clientele to great acclaim.
She currently resides in Germantown, Maryland, with her husband John, and their daughter, Mary Paige.

This edition published by Barnes & Noble, Inc., by arrangement with Random House Value Publishing, Inc.

ISBN 0-7607-15998

1999 Barnes & Noble Books

Printed and bound in the United States of America

Table of Contents

Introduction

What is a bread machine?

It is a futuristic-looking kitchen appliance about the size of a small microwave oven that does virtually all the work that the world's best bread bakers do by hand.

More specifically, it is a machine with a removable metal pail, kneading hook, and heating coil all built-in to make nutritious homemade bread as easily as it is to prepare a bowl of cereal. You need only to pour ingredients into the pail, close the lid and hit a button in order to have fresh, hot homemade bread within 2–4 hours. The machine does the mixing and kneading, times the rises and rests, and bakes the bread with no further effort on your part.

If you are in a hurry, most machines have a "quick" setting for making breads faster, often by using rapid rise yeast.

On the other hand, if you would like to wake up to a fragrant, crusty loaf on Sunday morning, you may put the ingredients in Saturday night and set the timer for your wake-up time, say, noon.

And if you would rather shape the loaves yourself, or make pizza dough, pretzels, bagels, etc., you may use the "dough" setting to knead and rise your mixture.

Sounds like a nice luxury, you say, but how *important* is it? For people with health considerations or dietary restrictions it could be very important. Store-bought breads routinely contain high amounts of sodium and corn syrup. Do calcium propionate, sodium diacetate, acetic acid and lactic acid sound appetizing to you? You will find them in virtually *all* the wrapped bread at the grocery store . . . and also in the cosmetic section in hair dyes and freckle bleaching creams. If you get these chemicals on your hands, they may cause mild to severe irritation. Acetic acid, in particular, is highly corrosive and its vapors can cause lung obstruction. Furthermore, it has been conclusively proven to cause cancer.

Homemade bread contains only flour, water, butter, yeast, and small amounts of sugar and salt. Perhaps fruit or cheese. Even peanut butter and jelly—whatever *you* want. And for those allergic to wheat flour, other flours, such as oat, can be used.

You can make a choice!

Until now, though, it was difficult and time-consuming to make bread at home, particularly for people who worked all day or who had small children—exactly the people who need healthy foods the most. Now, with a bread machine, anyone can make one, two, or even three or more loaves of bread a day almost effortlessly!

I have compiled my own recipes—for sandwich, savory and dessert loaves—into this volume. Some of them are traditional, some are more creative and fanciful. Some are perfect for a romantic tryst in the French countryside with ripe cheeses and a jug of wine; others are more suited to feed a finicky toddler a balanced meal-in-one in a suburban kitchen. Some, as indicated by asterisks, are dairy-free, making them safe for those allergic to milk products. Every one of them has been tested—for taste, ease and convenience—by myself and other bread machine owners. All of the following recipes make a good one-pound loaf in virtually any make of bread machine.

Enjoy!

Ideas and Hints for Using Your Bread Machine

1. Keep a large plastic mixing bowl just for your bread-making tools. Store measuring spoons, measuring cups, etc. inside the bowl, so when it's time to make bread it's all right there. You can even mix the ingredients in the bowl before you put them in the machine.

2. If you make a lot of one bread, mix the staple ingredients together in a container (1 part salt, 1 part sugar, 2 parts nonfat dry milk powder) so that you don't have to search them out every time.

I have a friend who uses a large Rubbermaid® bucket with a lid and mixes in the correct proportions of flour, sugar, salt, milk powder and active dry yeast so that all she has to do to make her favorite white bread is add water. A dry mixture like this will last several weeks tightly covered and kept in a cool place (preferably the refrigerator).

3. If you need to measure and pour an ingredient that is very sticky (like peanut butter), swirl some vegetable oil around in your measuring cup first, pour it out, then measure the sticky ingredient in the lubricated cup.

4. If you are using the timer, make sure that the yeast and the milk powder are at the bottom of the pan, farthest from the liquid.

5. If you have a machine that makes round loaves (or even if you don't) you can make bread "bowls" for soups by slicing off the crusty, bowled top and hollowing it to about one-quarter inch. Whole wheat breads and thick bisques work particularly well together.

6. Please remember that ingredients are not strictly predictable. Altitude, age, settling and a lot of other factors can

have one cup of whole wheat flour need ½ cup of water to make dough while another might need a whole cup. Take a peek at your dough while it's kneading; if it's terribly thin and sticky, add a tablespoon of flour at a time until it's smooth and elastic and only slightly sticky to the touch. On the other hand, if the dough is very stiff, add a tablespoon of water one at a time until it becomes more pliable.

IMPORTANT: Unless your bread machine instructions specifically instruct you NOT to open the machine while it's kneading, it's just fine to open it and look at the dough during any part of the process except baking (when too much heat would escape). The variation in altitudes and freshness of ingredients can affect your bread dramatically, so you MUST check the dough at least the first few times you use the machine, in order to see how dry or sticky is ideal for baking.

Also, if a dough looks too liquidy do not stop the machine and take the baking pan out—just let it bake through. Otherwise, you could spill the batter all over the workings of your machine, especially if you have one of the brands with a hole in the bottom of the baking pan.

7. The recipes in this book make one-pound loaves of bread. If your machine happens to make 1½-pound loaves, increase the dry ingredients by one cup (or in like proportion to what's already in the recipe) and increase the liquid by four ounces (½ cup). In very dense loaves, you may want to double the yeast, but it's not necessary.

8. Many common recipes create two 1½-pound loaves, so you can generally adapt it by using a third of the ingredients. Take your cues from the amount of flour called for—a bread machine will generally accommodate 2–3 cups.

9. Most of the breads in this book can be made by hand, by following the general directions for breadmaking: knead the ingredients for at least ten minutes, grease a bowl and put the dough ball in. Cover loosely with a towel or cloth. Let the

dough rise until doubled in bulk—about 1½ hours. Punch it down, turn it out on a floured board and knead for 3–5 more minutes. Shape it, and let it rise until doubled again, about an hour. Bake at 375 degrees for 50 minutes to an hour, or until the bread sounds hollow when you knock on the top.

10. Finally, one of the great things about a bread machine is that you can make some very tender breads in it that you couldn't make by hand because the dough isn't firm enough for traditional kneading. Remember that most of the time a loose dough bakes into a fine, tender loaf.

11. In any recipe marked with an asterisk (*) indicating dairy-free, you may substitute water for milk and/or margarine for butter. In fact, you can *always* substitute butter with margarine.

12. You may contact the author of this book with any questions or comments via e-mail: EHarbison@AOL.com

Yeast

Yeast is a living, single-cell organism which feeds on sugar, converting it to carbon dioxide. What does this mean in breadmaking? Simply put, when you mix sugar and yeast into your dough, the yeast expells gas, puffing the dough with air and making it rise. This is the main reason bread recipes call for natural sweeteners.

Generally recipes will also call for salt. Salt slows the action of the yeast so that your loaves won't rise too high and then collapse. It also brings out the full flavor of the bread.

Sugar and salt used in the small amounts necessary to provide yeast action are not, generally speaking, very big factors in diet. The amounts do change from one recipe to another for flavor reasons, and if there is more of one ingredient than you feel comfortable with, decrease it. Experiment.

There are three kinds of baker's yeast that you can use for breadmaking. They are:

1. *Compressed Fresh Yeast*—comes in cakes of either .06 ounces, 1 ounce, or 2 ounces. I buy the smallest (.06 ounces) and use one cake as the equivalent of one (1/4-ounce) package or envelope of active dry yeast.

Because compressed fresh yeast is so moist, it perishes very quickly, usually lasting only 1–2 weeks. Check the expiration date on the package. If you have any questions, it's a good idea to test it (known as "proofing") before adding it to a recipe.

Compressed fresh yeast can be frozen with good results. But you must be sure to defrost it at room temperature and use it right away.

Too much trouble? Some people prefer the convenience of dry yeasts, but compressed yeast makes a noticeable improvement in flavor. It also improves the nutritional content and lasting quality of the bread.

2. *Active Dry Yeast*—comes in small envelopes, usually three to a package, containing 1/4 ounce (or 1 tablespoon) of yeast. These envelopes are sealed, so the yeast is alive but dormant until it is revived in warm liquid. Unopened packages of active dry yeast may last 6–10 months, but do check the expiration date on the crimp.

You may also buy active dry yeast in 4-ounce jars, or even in bulk from health food stores. Because large quantities of unsealed yeast expires quickly, however, it's a good idea to proof it before you use it.

Active dry yeast has a good flavor, although not quite as good as compressed yeast. The bread will last fairly well.

3. *Quick-Rising Yeast*—comes in 1/4-ounce envelopes. One brand calls it "rapid rise" yeast. It's used in the same way as active dry yeast, but it works in about half the time.

Quick-rising yeast has a rather bland flavor; bread made with it will have a short shelf life (only a couple of days).

Proofing the Yeast

If you are unsure as to the freshness of your yeast, you must proof, or test it to make sure it is still active. Otherwise, you may have a loaf that won't rise and you will have wasted all of your other ingredients—not to mention precious time.

Usually, you can be fairly sure the yeast is good if you are within the expiration period marked on the package. Some people like to proof it anyway, and that's fine. But often I will use the yeast without proofing it and rarely have a problem.

If you are making a bread in which water is an ingredient, you're in luck when it comes to proofing. Heat the water to 100–115 degrees or as low as 80 degrees for fresh yeast (use a cooking thermometer the first few times, so that you get to know what the right temperature feels like), add a pinch of sugar and your yeast. Wait five to ten minutes and the yeast should become bubbly and frothy on top. If it doesn't, it's dead and it should be discarded.

If the bread that you're making does *not* contain water, then you may proof the yeast in a small amount of water, compensating by using less milk or other liquid in the recipe. Or you may proof just a little bit of yeast from your package, saving the rest for your bread. This is a good way to proof yeast you are using for timed breads.

It's been my experience that it doesn't usually make a lot of difference how much yeast you use—so if you're a pinch under or a pinch over, don't worry.

Ingredient Information

- *All-Purpose Flour*—Made from a blend of high-gluten hard wheat and low-gluten soft wheat, and contains neither wheat germ nor bran. This is perfectly adequate flour for bread, though for lighter loaves, bread flour is preferable. All-purpose flour comes bleached and unbleached—unbleached is better for you unless you know with certainty that the bleaching method was natural (most are chemical).

- *Arrowroot*—Used as a thickener or to prevent dough from sticking.

- *Barley Flour*—Very low in gluten (protein) and must be used in conjunction with higher-gluten flours (such as bread or whole wheat) or with an added tablespoon of whole wheat gluten, which is available in most health food stores. Barley flour imparts a sweet, nutty flavor.

- *Bread Flour*—A blend of 99.8% hard wheat flour and a small amount of malted barley flour (to enhance the yeast activity) and potassium bromate (to enhance the rising action of the dough). This is the flour of choice for making light, fluffy loaves. Like all-purpose flour, it contains neither the wheat germ nor the bran.

- *Butter*—I prefer unsalted butter to margarine because I feel it's a more pure, wholesome product. Although a common misconception, butter is no more fattening than margarine. It does, however, contain saturated fats and cholesterol; for that reason many people prefer margarine. Margarine, or even soy margarine, may be used in place of butter in all of these recipes. It must be melted, then cooled before using.

- *Cornstarch*—Used as a thickener or to prevent dough from sticking.

- *Cracked Wheat*—Composed of crushed wheat berries which have been toasted to a crisp texture. Cracked wheat must be soaked for at least an hour before it is used for bread. You may soak it, drain it, and add it to your ingredients or, if you're using the timer, simply put the cracked wheat in last, on top of the liquid.

- *Eggs*—You may use no-cholesterol egg substitutes (which can be found in the frozen breakfast section of your grocery store) or egg powder in place of eggs. Use lightly beaten eggs unless otherwise specified.

- *Enriched Flour*—This has lost nutrients in the milling process, thus been enriched with iron, thiamine, riboflavin, and niacin. Contrary to popular belief, "enriched" does not mean that the flour is not nutritious.

- *Gluten*—The high-protein hard flour that is left when the starch is rinsed from whole wheat flour. It's the gluten in flour that helps hold the carbon dioxide released by the yeast. Gluten is necessary for a well-risen loaf. Bread flour, all-purpose flour, and whole wheat flour are all "high gluten" flours, with enough gluten in them to make a fine loaf. Other flours, like rye and pastry, need the boost of either pure whole wheat gluten or the addition of a high-gluten flour.

- *Margarine*—A fine substitution for butter in all of these recipes.

- *Milk*—Makes bread soft and tender inside. You can use anything from skim milk to buttermilk. You can also substitute nonfat dry milk powder added to water to make the necessary amount. If you do this for timed breads, make sure that the milk powder, along with the yeast, is at the bottom, farthest away from the liquid.

- *Oats*—A very nutritious addition to breads because they are rich in protein and B-complex vitamins. For these recipes you may use either "quick" or "rolled" oats.

- *Oils*—You may use oil instead of butter or margarine in any recipe. When I call for "light vegetable oil" I mean canola oil, which is lower than others in polyunsaturates.

- *Rice Flour*—A very mild, low-gluten flour, which must be used in conjunction with either pure wheat gluten (1 tablespoon) or an equal amount of high-gluten flour like bread or whole wheat.

- *Rye Flour*—Tangy and pungent, it comes in light, medium and dark. The usual grocery store variety is medium, but you may use any variety, depending on how bitter you like your rye. Because it is low-gluten, it must be used in conjunction with either 1 tablespoon of whole wheat gluten, or with a high-gluten flour such as bread or whole wheat.

- *Salt*—Slows the yeast's action and helps add full-bodied flavor to the bread. Because it is used in small amounts for bread, it will not adversely affect one's diet.

- *Self-Rising Flour*—An all-purpose flour with added baking soda and salt. It is not the best flour for bread, but if you use it, compensate for its added sodium by omitting the salt in the recipe.

- *Soy Flour*—A very high-protein flour used in small amounts because of its strong flavor.

- *Sugar*—Like other sweeteners, such as brown sugar, molasses, honey, barley malt or corn syrup, sugar is necessary for the yeast to work. Without the sweetener, the yeast will not ferment or produce the gas that adds air to the dough so it will rise. Sugar substitutes, like saccharine or Nutrasweet®, will not do.

- *Water*—Gives the bread an excellent crust and may be used in place of milk in most recipes.
- *Wheat Germ*—Is high in protein, vitamins and minerals. It is also high in fat—which means that if it's not kept refrigerated it may turn rancid. Do not keep wheat germ longer than six months.
- *Whole Wheat Flour*—A stronger flavor than bread flour, it contains the wheat germ, making it higher in fiber, nutritional content, and fat. Because of the latter it should be stored in the refrigerator and used within six months.
- *Whole Wheat Gluten*—A greyish powder that may be used in small amounts to help a loaf that is composed largely of low-gluten flours. Whole wheat gluten is not difficult to find; most health food stores carry it.

White Breads

These are the breads most suited for lunchbox sandwiches, fondues, French toast, and simply toasted with butter.

White Bread

Do not discount this as "mere white bread." It is excellent to have on hand for a variety of uses. This is the one bread that you can almost count on everyone loving—it has a rich bread scent, tender middle, and nice brown crust.

It also has the added distinction of being the one recipe that you may experiment with pretty safely: almost anything tastes good mixed into white bread.

2 t or ½ package of yeast
2 c bread flour
1 T nonfat dry milk powder
1 t sugar
1 t salt
2 T butter
⅞ c water

Add all the ingredients to the machine in the order listed. Choose either regular or light crust (depending on your preference) and push "Start."

R This recipe will work on a "rapid" or "quick bread" setting.

T This bread may be prepared on the timer; if you use the timer method, though, use active dry yeast (rather than compressed) and if you have a yeast dispenser, use it!

Sally Lunn Bread

This is a nutritious white bread named for the young European girl who, in legend, sold it on street corners. Enjoy it as morning toast or use it to make a doubly nutritious French toast.

- 2 t or ½ package of yeast
- 2 c bread flour
- 2 T sugar
- 1 t salt
- 2 eggs
- 4 T + 2 t butter
- 3 T milk
- ⅓ c water

Add all the ingredients to the machine in the order listed. Choose either regular or light crust (depending on your preference) and push "Start."

R This recipe will work on a "rapid" or "quick bread" setting.

French Bread (Crusty)

This is the bread to make for fondue or to serve with cheese spreads. It's also delicious for breakfast, toasted and smothered with fruit preserves.

2 t or 1/2 package yeast
2 c bread flour
1 T + 1 t sugar
1 t salt
1 T + 1 t butter
7/8 c water
2 stiffly beaten egg whites

Beat the egg whites and set them aside. Put the remaining ingredients in your bread machine, in the order listed, and push "Start." When all the ingredients are moistened, add the egg whites.

For an even crisper crust

combine in a small bowl:

1 T water
1/4 t salt
1/4 t arrowroot or cornstarch

Brush this mixture on for the second rise. You may also sprinkle poppy seeds on at this time.

Potato Loaf Bread

This award-winning Pennsylvania Dutch bread is melt-in-your-mouth tender. Buttered, hot from the machine, it is delectable.

2 t or ½ package of yeast
2 c bread flour
1 T sugar
1½ t salt
1 T butter
¼ c instant mashed potato flakes
1 c warm milk

Put the first 5 ingredients into the bread machine's baking dish. Sprinkle the mashed potato flakes over the hot milk in a separate bowl and stir. Cool to warm and add to the ingredients in the dish and push "Start."

Sour Cream Bread

My sister used to make this bread by hand and it was always gone before it reached the table. The few times I attempted it by hand I found it very difficult. But the bread machine makes it perfectly. It's fantastic eaten hot from the machine, and buttered (it's even good without butter!).

2 t or ½ package of yeast
2 c bread flour
1 T sugar
½ t salt
⅛ t baking soda
1 c sour cream
¼ c water

Add all the ingredients to the machine in the order listed. Choose either regular or light crust (depending on your preference) and push "Start."

Honey Buttermilk Bread

Buttermilk gives this soft and chewy loaf a very rich flavor. Great for French toast or with jam for breakfast.

- 2 t or 1/2 package of yeast
- 2 c bread flour
- 1 1/2 t salt
- 3/4 c buttermilk (or 3/4 c milk to which you have added 1 t of vinegar or lemon juice)
- 2 T honey
- 1 T butter
- 3 T water

Add all the ingredients to the machine in the order listed. Choose either regular or light crust (depending on your preference) and push "Start."

Renaissance White Bread

Legend has it that this simple bread was sold on the streets of Rome in the Middle Ages.

2 t or ½ package yeast
2¼ c unbleached white flour
1 T sugar
2 t salt
3 T butter
1 c water

Add all the ingredients to the machine in the order listed. Choose either regular or light crust (depending on your preference) and push "Start."

English Muffin Bread

This is a tasty breakfast bread, ideally suited for toasting and buttering. It is sturdy enough to use in place of hamburger buns.

2 t or ½ package of yeast
2 c bread flour
1 t sugar
1 t salt
2 T nonfat dry milk powder
⅛ t baking soda
1 c minus 1 T water

Add all the ingredients to the machine in the order listed. Choose either regular or light crust (depending on your preference) and push "Start."

R The above recipes will work on a "rapid" or "quick bread" setting.

T The above breads may be prepared on the timer; if you use the timer method, though, use active dry yeast (rather than compressed) and if you have a yeast dispenser, use it!

Peasant Bread*

For years, this bread has been made and sold at fairs. Traditionally, it is baked, then fried in butter and sprinkled with powdered sugar . . . use your own discretion.

2 t or ½ package of yeast
2 c bread flour
1½ t sugar
1 t salt
⅞ c water

Add all the ingredients to the machine in the order listed. Choose either regular or light crust (depending on your preference) and push "Start."

* This recipe is dairy-free.

R This recipe will work on a "rapid" or "quick bread" setting.

T This bread may be prepared on the timer; if you use the timer method, though, use active dry yeast (rather than compressed) and if you have a yeast dispenser, use it!

Crusty White Bread

So simple and basic, yet so wonderful. Similar to Renaissance White Bread, but with less sugar, this white bread is great to use in recipes. It is nice in fondues or soups, such as French onion. It also makes good croutons: simply heat some olive oil and garlic in a skillet and gently fry small chunks of bread to put on salads and soups.

2 t or ½ package of yeast
2 c bread flour
2 t salt
1 t sugar
⅞ c water

Add all the ingredients to the machine in the order listed. Choose either regular or light crust (depending on your preference) and push "Start."

R This recipe will work on a "rapid" or "quick bread" setting.

T This bread may be prepared on the timer; if you use the timer method, though, use active dry yeast (rather than compressed) and if you have a yeast dispenser, use it!

French Country Bread*

Be aware that there are different grades of olive oil. I use "extra virgin" because it is more flavorful. Some people prefer lesser grades, though, since the scent of the olive oil is much less pronounced.

2 t or ½ package of yeast
2 c bread flour
⅔ t sugar
1 t salt
2 t olive oil
2 t honey
¾ c water

Add all the ingredients to the machine in the order listed. Choose either regular or light crust (depending on your preference) and push "Start."

* This recipe is dairy-free.

R This recipe will work on a "rapid" or "quick bread" setting.

T This bread may be prepared on the timer; if you use the timer method, though, use active dry yeast (rather than compressed) and if you have a yeast dispenser, use it!

French Bread (Tender)

This is a sweet, tender loaf that makes wonderful European-style breakfast toast. This bread has a very liquidy dough but will bake to a firm loaf.

- 2 t or ½ package of yeast
- 2 c bread flour
- 1 t salt
- 1 t sugar
- 1 t butter
- ¼ c nonfat dry milk powder
- 1 c plus 1 T warm water

Add all the ingredients to the machine in the order listed. Choose either regular or light crust (depending on your preference) and push "Start."

Italian Bread

This bread is particularly nice when it's cut into bite-sized chunks and served with sharp cheese and red wine—and in the company of good friends, of course.

- 2 t or ½ package of yeast
- 2 c bread flour
- 1 t sugar
- 1 t salt
- 2 T mild white vinegar
- ⅔ c water

Add all the ingredients to the machine in the order listed. Choose either regular or light crust (depending on your preference) and push "Start."

R The above recipes aboye will work on a "rapid" or "quick bread" setting.

T The above breads may be prepared on the timer; if you use the timer method, though, use active dry yeast (rather than compressed) and if you have a yeast dispenser, use it!

Malt Bread

The malt in this recipe gives the bread a mellow, slightly sweet flavor. You can find malt powder in the grocery store, near the chocolate milk and hot cocoa mixes. Carnation® makes a very good one. Unless you want to experiment, make sure you get "plain," rather than "chocolate" flavored malt.

2 t or ½ package of yeast
2 c bread flour
1 T sugar
1 T salt
3 T malted milk powder
2 T butter
⅔ c water

Add all the ingredients to the machine in the order listed. Choose either regular or light crust (depending on your preference) and push "Start."

T This bread may be prepared on the timer; if you use the timer method, though, use active dry yeast (rather than compressed) and if you have a yeast dispenser, use it!

Buttermilk Bread

Buttermilk is the liquid left over when butter has been churned. Pioneer women were loathe to waste anything so they would use the buttermilk to make this tasty, light-textured bread.

- 2 t or ½ package of yeast
- 2 c bread flour
- ⅔ t sugar
- ⅔ t salt
- 2 T butter
- ⅔ c buttermilk (or ⅔ c of milk to which you have added 1 t vinegar or lemon juice)

Add all the ingredients to the machine in the order listed. Choose either regular or light crust (depending on your preference) and push "Start."

Hominy Bread

Hominy was one of the first foods the American Indians gave to the colonial settlers. They ate it plain, heated and mixed with water like gruel, and also as a healthy bread. This is good with stews, or as a side dish for fried chicken.

- 2 t or ½ package of yeast
- 2 c bread flour
- 1 c cooked hominy grits ("instant" is fine—prepare 2 envelopes)
- 2 t sugar
- ½ t salt
- 1 T butter
- 2 T water

Add all the ingredients to the machine in the order listed. Choose either regular or light crust (depending on your preference) and push "Start."

Anadama Bread

Lore has it that the name "Anadama" comes from the New England farmer who invented this early American bread. When he tired of the cornmeal gruel his wife served him every night, he added yeast and flour to it and, stirring with a vengeance, repeated "Anna, damn her! Anna, damn her!"

2 t or 1/2 package of yeast
2 c bread flour
2 1/2 T cornmeal
2 1/2 T molasses
1/2 t salt
1 T butter
1 c + 2 t water

Add all the ingredients to the machine in the order listed. Choose either regular or light crust (depending on your preference) and push "Start."

Beer Bread*

This recipe makes a tender bread with a good crust. It's delicious for sandwiches or just toasted with butter. For a denser loaf you may substitute 1/2 cup of whole wheat flour for 1/2 cup of the bread flour.

2 t or 1/2 package of yeast
2 c bread flour
1 T sugar
3/4 t salt
1 T margarine (or butter)
1 c warm beer or ale

Add all the ingredients to the machine in the order listed. Choose either regular or light crust (depending on your preference) and push "Start."

* This recipe is dairy-free.

Cheese Breads

*Wonderful, all of them,
and virtually guaranteed to make
a hit at parties. Eat them plain,
or toasted with butter.*

Cheese and Onion Bread

This bread is so flavorful that you may want to have it simply plain or toasted. It is a delightful addition to the picnic basket in summer or enjoyed with a hearty winter soup in cold weather.

2 t or ½ package of yeast
2 c bread flour
1 T sugar
1 t salt
½ c small curd cottage cheese
½ c grated sharp cheddar cheese
1 egg
1 T butter
3 T grated onion
2 T toasted sesame seeds
¾ c water

Add all the ingredients to the machine in the order listed. Choose either regular or light crust (depending on your preference) and push "Start."

Beer Cheese Bread

This flavorful, crusty cheese bread is my favorite.

- 2 t or ½ package of yeast
- 2 c bread flour
- 1 T sugar
- 1½ t salt
- 1 T butter
- 1 c beer
- ½ c shredded sharp cheddar cheese
- ½ c shredded Jack cheese

Warm butter in saucepan to just melted. Add beer, cheddar and Jack cheese and stir until cheese starts to melt. Take off heat.

Add all the ingredients to the machine in the order listed. Choose either regular or light crust (depending on your preference) and push "Start."

Buttermilk Cheese Bread

This is a tender, flaky bread that melts in your mouth. If you like blue cheese, it can be used as an excellent substitute for a portion of the sharp cheddar cheese.

2 t or ½ package of yeast
2 c bread flour
1 t baking powder
1 t salt
1 T sugar
1 c buttermilk
1 c grated sharp cheddar (or ½ c each blue cheese and cheddar)

Add all the ingredients to the machine in the order listed. Choose either regular or light crust (depending on your preference) and push "Start."

Cottage Cheese Bread

This is a nutritious bread to eat when you're on the run. It's also great for making French toast.

2 t or ½ package of yeast
2 c bread flour
2 t sugar
⅔ t salt
⅛ teaspoon baking soda
1 egg
2 T butter
⅔ c cottage cheese
⅔ c water

Add all the ingredients to the machine in the order listed. Choose either regular or light crust (depending on your preference) and push "Start."

Farmer's Cheese Bread

This is a favorite in our household. I like to serve it buttered, with lasagne.

2 t or ½ package of yeast
2 c bread flour
2 T sugar
1 t salt
1 egg
2 T butter
⅓ c milk
1 c farmer's or ricotta cheese

Add all the ingredients to the machine in the order listed. Choose either regular or light crust (depending on your preference) and push "Start."

Cheddar Cheese Bread

The sharper the cheese, the better the bread. Add the cheese after the first kneading, or after the indicator beep (if your machine has one).

2 t or ½ package of yeast	1 t butter
2 c flour	⅔ c milk
2 t sugar	¾ c shredded cheddar cheese
½ t salt	

Add all the ingredients to the machine in the order listed. Choose either regular or light crust (depending on your preference) and push "Start."

Egg and Cheese Bread

Using eggs in this bread makes it extra nutritious, moist, and chewy. This is one of the best cheese breads, excellent for breakfast.

2 t or ½ package of yeast	4 T + 2 t butter
2 c bread flour	½ c shredded sharp cheddar
2 T sugar	¼ c milk
1 t salt	½ c water
2 eggs	

Add all the ingredients to the machine in the order listed. Choose either regular or light crust (depending on your preference) and push "Start."

Cream Cheese Bread

The cream cheese makes this a mildly tangy bread that is excellent served with white wine. Weight-conscious eaters can substitute Neufchôtel cheese or "light" cream cheese for the cream cheese.

- 2 t or ½ package of yeast
- 2 c bread flour
- 1 T sugar
- 1 t salt
- 1 egg
- 2 T butter
- ⅔ c cream cheese
- 3 T nonfat dry milk powder
- ⅔ c water

Add all the ingredients to the machine in the order listed. Choose either regular or light crust (depending on your preference) and push "Start."

Three Cheese Bread

This makes a moist and cheesy loaf—so good it can stand on its own, but sinful with butter.

- 2 t or ½ package of yeast
- 2 c bread flour
- 2 T sugar
- 1 t salt
- 2 eggs
- 2 T butter
- 1 c ricotta cheese
- ½ c shredded sharp cheddar
- ½ c grated parmesan
- ⅓ c milk

Add all the ingredients to the machine in the order listed. Choose either regular or light crust (depending on your preference) and push "Start."

Tomato and Cheese Bread

This makes excellent cheese sandwiches and is especially delicious with tomato soup.

- 2 t or ½ package of yeast
- 2 c bread flour
- 1 T nonfat dry milk powder
- 1 t sugar
- 1 t salt
- 2 T butter
- ¾ c shredded sharp cheddar cheese
- ⅞ c tomato juice

Add all the ingredients to the machine in the order listed. Choose either regular or light crust (depending on your preference) and push "Start."

Parmesan Herb Loaf

My friend Lucinda invented this bread for her bread machine and we enjoyed it a great deal one evening on her deck. Since then, I have made it frequently, often for guests, and the recipe never fails. You can use absolutely any herbs, in any combination.

- 2 t or ½ package of yeast
- 2 c bread flour
- 1 T nonfat dry milk powder
- 1 t sugar
- 1 t salt
- 2 T butter
- ⅞ c water
- ½ c grated parmesan cheese
- 1 T mixed herbs

Add all the ingredients to the machine in the order listed. Choose either regular or light crust (depending on your preference) and push "Start."

T This bread may be prepared on the timer; if you use the timer method, though, use active dry yeast (rather than compressed) and be sure to put it in the yeast dispenser.

Parmesan Garlic Loaf

Perfect with spaghetti. Make the bread in your machine and serve it plain or buttered. If you are feeling extra decadent, slice it, butter the slices, sprinkle them with garlic powder and bake them in the oven for several minutes before serving. The smell is heavenly!

2 t or ½ package of yeast
2 c bread flour
⅔ t sugar
¾ t salt
½ c grated parmesan cheese
4 cloves garlic, minced
1 T Italian Herbs mix (optional)
⅞ c water

Add all the ingredients to the machine in the order listed. Choose either regular or light crust (depending on your preference) and push "Start."

R This recipe will work on a "rapid" or "quick bread" setting.

T This bread may be prepared on the timer; if you use the timer method, though, use active dry yeast (rather than compressed) and if you have a yeast dispenser, use it!

Oregano Parmesan Cheese Bread

Another excellent side bread for Italian dishes. Use some caution with the oregano—the taste can sometimes be very strong.

2 t or 1/2 package yeast
2 c bread flour
3 T nonfat dry milk powder
2 t dried oregano leaves
1/4 c grated parmesan cheese
1 t sugar
1 1/2 t salt
2 T olive oil
7/8 c water

Add all the ingredients to the machine in the order listed. Choose either regular or light crust (depending on your preference) and push "Start."

Corn Dog Bread

Children, the primary consumers of corn dogs at fairs, love this bread, making it a good, if sneaky way to give a finicky child a "meal in one." In order to keep the sliced franks somewhat whole, add them at the end of the first kneading. Don't worry about cooking them first, they'll bake along with the bread. Vegetarians may use textured vegetable protein franks or sausage links in place of the hot dogs.

2 t or ½ package of yeast
3 c bread flour
¼ t ginger
¼ t sugar
½ c corn meal
2 t mustard seeds
1 t salt
1 t sugar
½ c grated sharp cheddar cheese
2 T hot salsa
1 egg
3 T sweet pickle relish
1 T vegetable oil
1 c warm water
1 c sliced franks

Add all the ingredients to the machine in the order listed. Choose either regular or light crust (depending on your preference) and push "Start."

Whole Grain, Nut and Seed Breads

These super-healthy breads provide nutrition and fiber to your diet and energy to your life. Use whole grain breads for hearty sandwiches, croutons, and toast.

Whole Wheat Bread

This is light and delicious enough to use for children's lunchbox sandwiches. An added bonus: no complaints!

- 2 t or ½ package of yeast
- 2 c bread flour
- 1 c whole wheat flour
- 2 T sugar
- 2 t salt
- ¼ c nonfat dry milk powder
- 1 egg
- ¼ c (½ stick) butter
- 1 c water

Add all the ingredients to the machine in the order listed. Choose either regular or light crust (depending on your preference) and push "Start."

R This recipe will work on a "rapid" or "quick bread" setting.

T This bread may be prepared on the timer; if you use the timer method, though, use active dry yeast (rather than compressed) and if you have a yeast dispenser, use it!

Honey Wheat Germ Bread

This is a slightly sweet, hearty bread that is great for sandwiches. This bread has a very liquidy dough. If, however, you want to stiffen it up a little, add white flour—one tablespoon at a time—until you have the consistency you prefer.

2 t or 1/2 package of yeast
1 1/2 c bread flour
3/4 c whole wheat flour
1/4 c wheat germ
1 T brown sugar
1/2 t salt
3 T nonfat dry milk powder
1/4 c honey
1 1/4 c water

Add all the ingredients to the machine in the order listed. Choose either regular or light crust (depending on your preference) and push "Start."

R This recipe will work on a "rapid" or "quick bread" setting.

T This bread may be prepared on the timer; if you use the timer method, though, use active dry yeast (rather than compressed) and if you have a yeast dispenser, use it!

Seed Bread

Thanks in large part to the combination of nuts and seeds, this is a super-energy bread, perfect for getting started in the morning. Makes a complete meal with just a glass of milk.

- 2 t or ½ package of yeast
- 1 c bread flour
- 1 c whole wheat flour
- ½ c light rye flour
- ½ c cornmeal
- ½ c unprocessed bran
- 1 t salt
- ⅓ c raisins
- ⅓ c chopped pecans or walnuts
- ⅓ c sunflower seeds
- ⅓ c poppy seeds
- 2 T caraway seeds
- 4 T honey
- 1 egg
- 1 c water
- ⅓ c milk
- 1 T light vegetable oil

Add all the ingredients to the machine in the order listed. Choose either regular or light crust (depending on your preference) and push "Start."

Maple Oatmeal Bread*

This New England bread dates back to colonial times— as so many maple syrup recipes do.

2 t or 1/2 package of yeast
1 c quick oats
2 c bread flour
1 t salt
1/3 c pure maple syrup
1 T light vegetable oil
1 c water

Add all the ingredients to the machine in the order listed. Choose either regular or light crust (depending on your preference) and push "Start."

* This recipe is dairy-free.

R This recipe will work on a "rapid" or "quick bread" setting.

T This bread may be prepared on the timer; if you use the timer method, though, use active dry yeast (rather than compressed) and if you have a yeast dispenser, use it!

Raisin Bran Bread*

This makes terrific cinnamon toast!

2 t or ½ package of yeast
2 c bread flour
1 c raisin bran cereal
½ t salt
¼ t baking soda
4 T brown sugar
2 T margarine (or butter)
1 c water (or milk, if you are not avoiding dairy foods)

Add all the ingredients to the machine in the order listed. Choose either regular or light crust (depending on your preference) and push "Start."

* This recipe is dairy-free.

R This recipe will work on a "rapid" or "quick bread" setting.

T This bread may be prepared on the timer; if you use the timer method, though, use active dry yeast (rather than compressed) and if you have a yeast dispenser, use it!

Russian Black Bread*

This is a bittersweet bread with a rich and varied history. This particular recipe is an adaptation of a private one belonging to an acquaintance's old-world grandmother.

2 t or 1/2 package of yeast
1 c bread flour
1 c medium rye flour
1/4 c whole wheat flour
1/2 c unprocessed bran flakes
1 T caraway seeds
1 T sugar
1 t salt

1 t instant coffee granules
1/4 t fennel seeds
1 1/4 c water
2 T molasses
2 T cider vinegar
2 T margarine (or butter)
1/2 oz unsweetened chocolate

Place the water, molasses, vinegar, butter and chocolate over low heat to melt. Remove from heat and when cooled to lukewarm, add this mixture to the other ingredients in the baking dish. Push "Start."

* This recipe is dairy-free.

Yogurt Oatmeal Wheat Bread

Doesn't it just sound *nutritious?*

The oats and yogurt combine to make a fine, moist-textured bread.

- 2 t or ½ package of yeast
- 1½ c bread flour
- ½ c quick oats
- ¾ c whole wheat flour
- 2 t sugar
- 2 t salt
- 1 c plain yogurt
- 2 T butter
- ¾ c water

Add all the ingredients to the machine in the order listed. Choose either regular or light crust (depending on your preference) and push "Start."

Bran Bread*

You can use wheat bran, oat bran, or rice bran for this bread. It's fabulous toasted with jam on top.

- 2 t or ½ package of yeast
- 1½ c bread flour
- ½ c whole wheat flour
- 1 c bran
- ¼ c wheat germ
- 1 T brown sugar
- 1 t salt
- 2 T margarine (or butter)
- 1 c water

Add all the ingredients to the machine in the order listed. Choose either regular or light crust (depending on your preference) and push "Start."

* This recipe is dairy-free.

Diet Wheat Bread

Bread is never really very fattening, but some contain more shortening than others, thereby "sneaking" fat in. This has only ten grams of fat in the whole loaf.

2 t or ½ package of yeast
1 c bread flour
1 c whole wheat flour
1 T honey
1 t salt
1 T butter
3 T nonfat dry milk powder
1 c water

Add all the ingredients to the machine in the order listed. Choose either regular or light crust (depending on your preference) and push "Start."

R This recipe will work on a "rapid" or "quick bread" setting.

T This bread may be prepared on the timer; if you use the timer method, though, use active dry yeast (rather than compressed) and if you have a yeast dispenser, use it!

Cracked Wheat Bread*

If you find that the loaf is too dense, and you don't have gluten, you can try using an egg and a pinch of baking soda. If you use egg, however, remember to omit ¼ cup of water for each egg used.

- 3 t or 1 package of yeast
- 1½ c bread flour
- 1 c whole wheat flour
- 1 T honey
- 1 t salt
- 2 T light vegetable oil
- ½ c cracked wheat (or bulgur wheat)
- 1¼ c water

Add all the ingredients to the machine in the order listed. Choose either regular or light crust (depending on your preference) and push "Start."

* This recipe is dairy-free.

R This recipe will work on a "rapid" or "quick bread" setting.

T This bread may be prepared on the timer; if you use the timer method, though, use active dry yeast (rather than compressed) and if you have a yeast dispenser, use it!

High Protein Bread

This bread is based on Cornell University's "Triple Protein" formula. It's a good idea, especially for health-conscious parents, to mix 1 tablespoon each (or any equal amount that can be stored) of wheat germ, soy powder and dry milk powder and add 3 tablespoons of the mixture to every cup of flour you use. Many people add this formula to every flour they use, from pancakes to bread.

2 t or 1/2 package of yeast
1 c bread flour
1 c whole wheat flour
1/4 c soy flour
1/4 c nonfat dry milk powder
1/4 c wheat germ
1 T honey
1 t salt
1 T light vegetable oil
1 c water

Add all the ingredients to the machine in the order listed. Choose either regular or light crust (depending on your preference) and push "Start."

T If you use water instead of milk, you can use the timer for this recipe. Make sure that you use dry yeast (rather then compressed) and be sure to put it in the yeast dispenser, if you have one.

Multi-Grain Bread

Note the additional yeast in this bread; gluten is also helpful for making this loaf rise. Whether you use gluten or not, prepared and baked, it makes for a very heavy, dense loaf, packed with nutrition. Serve with winter soups and stews.

3 t or 1 package yeast
1 1/2 c bread flour
1/2 c rye flour
1/2 c bran
2 T wheat germ
1/4 c bulgur wheat (or cracked wheat)
1/4 c quick oats
1/4 c nonfat dry milk powder
2 T honey
1 1/2 t salt
3 T light vegetable oil
1 1/4 c water

Add all the ingredients to the machine in the order listed. Choose either regular or light crust (depending on your preference) and push "Start."

Buckwheat Bread

The buckwheat flour adds a very strong flavor. If you find it's too much, you can halve it and compensate with an additional ¼ cup of bread or whole wheat flour.

- 2 t or ½ package of yeast
- 1 c bread flour
- ¾ c whole wheat flour
- ½ c buckwheat flour
- 3 T nonfat dry milk powder
- 1 T honey
- 1 t salt
- 1 T vegetable oil
- 1 c water

Add all the ingredients to the machine in the order listed. Choose either regular or light crust (depending on your preference) and push "Start."

Whole Wheat Oatmeal Bread

The dry milk powder makes this bread surprisingly tender inside.

- 2 t or ½ package of yeast
- 1 c bread flour
- ¾ c whole wheat flour
- ½ c quick oats
- ¼ c wheat germ
- 2 T sugar
- 1½ t salt
- ¼ c nonfat dry milk powder
- 1 egg
- ¼ c (½ stick) butter
- ⅞ c water

Add all the ingredients to the machine in the order listed. Choose either regular or light crust (depending on your preference) and push "Start."

Oatmeal Bread

This is a traditional favorite. You may like to sprinkle some extra oats on top after the second kneading and before baking.

2 t or ½ package yeast	4 T butter
2 c bread flour	1 c buttermilk (or 1 cup milk with 1 t vinegar or lemon juice stirred in)
1 c quick oats	
2 T sugar	
1½ t salt	

Add all the ingredients to the machine in the order listed. Choose either regular or light crust (depending on your preference) and push "Start."

R This recipe will work on a "rapid" or "quick bread" setting.

T This bread may be prepared on the timer; if you use the timer method, though, use active dry yeast (rather than compressed) and if you have a yeast dispenser, use it!

Honey Nut Oat Bread

This is a delightful, slightly sweet, nutty bread. Makes very nice cinnamon toast.

2 t or ½ package of yeast
1½ c bread flour
½ c whole wheat flour
1 c quick oats
3 T nonfat dry milk powder
2 T honey
1 t salt
2 T light vegetable oil
1 c water

Add all the ingredients to the machine in the order listed. Choose either regular or light crust (depending on your preference) and push "Start."

After the first kneading add:

½ c chopped nuts (I use almonds or walnuts)

Grape Nuts® Bread*

This bread is terrific for peanut butter and jelly sandwiches.

- 2 t or ½ package of yeast
- 2 c bread flour
- ½ c Grape Nuts® cereal
- 1 T sugar
- 1½ t salt
- 2 T vegetable oil
- 1 cup water

Add all the ingredients to the machine in the order listed. Choose either regular or light crust (depending on your preference) and push "Start."

* This recipe is dairy-free.

R This recipe will work on a "rapid" or "quick bread" setting.

T This bread may be prepared on the timer; if you use the timer method, though, use active dry yeast (rather than compressed) and if you have a yeast dispenser, use it!

Rice Bread*

It is no coincidence that rice is the staple food for more than half the population of the world. It's an excellent source of complex carbohydrates and also calcium, iron and B-complex vitamins. Studies have shown that rice bran is as effective as oat bran in lowering cholesterol.

- 2 t or ½ package of yeast
- 2 c bread flour
- ½ c rice flour
- ½ c rice bran
- 1 T sugar
- 1 t salt
- 2 T margarine (or butter)
- 1 c water

Add all the ingredients to the machine in the order listed. Choose either regular or light crust (depending on your preference) and push "Start."

* This recipe is dairy-free.

R This recipe will work on a "rapid" or "quick bread" setting.

T This bread may be prepared on the timer; if you use the timer method, though, use active dry yeast (rather than compressed) and if you have a yeast dispenser, use it!

Barley Bread

The use of barley dates back to the Stone Age. Today it is primarily used to make beer and whiskey, but it is also used in cereals and breads. Try this bread for a hearty sandwich and enjoy it with a mug of ale.

2 t or ½ package of yeast
2½ c bread flour
½ c barley flour
1½ T nonfat dry milk powder
⅓ c sugar
1½ t salt
1 t cinamon
3 T molasses, either dark or light
2 T butter
1 c water

Add all the ingredients to the machine in the order listed. Choose either regular or light crust (depending on your preference) and push "Start."

T This bread may be prepared on the timer; if you use the timer method, though, use active dry yeast (rather than compressed) and if you have a yeast dispenser, use it!

Sunflower Seed Bread

Sunflower seeds give you energy—lots of it! They are rich in iron and protein, making this a very good choice for breakfast bread. Prepare it on the timer so it's ready when you wake up.

2 t or ½ package of yeast
1 c bread flour
1 c whole wheat flour
3 T nonfat dry milk powder
¼ c shelled sunflower seeds
1 T light vegetable oil
1 T honey
1 t salt
1 c water

Add all the ingredients to the machine in the order listed. Choose either regular or light crust (depending on your preference) and push "Start."

R This recipe will work on a "rapid" or "quick bread" setting.

T This bread may be prepared on the timer; if you use the timer method, though, use active dry yeast (rather than compressed) and if you have a yeast dispenser, use it!

Irish Soda Bread

After the second rise, take a knife and quickly slash a cross in the top of the bread. Although it doesn't necessarily enhance the quality of the bread, the slash is traditionally done to scare the devil away!

2 t or 1/2 package yeast	1 T sugar
2 c bread flour	2/3 t salt
1 t caraway seeds	1 T butter
1/3 t baking soda	2/3 c buttermilk

Add all the ingredients to the machine in the order listed. Choose either regular or light crust (depending on your preference) and push "Start."

After the first kneading, or after the indicator beep, add:

1/3 c currants or raisins

R This recipe will work on a "rapid" or "quick bread" setting.

Granola Bread

You may use any granola for this recipe—homemade, "natural cereal," with or without fruit, with or without nuts . . . whatever you prefer.

2 t or ½ package of yeast
1½ c bread flour
½ c whole wheat flour
½ c granola, finely ground in a food processor or blender
1 t sugar
1 t salt
2 T butter
2 T honey
1 egg
½ c buttermilk
¼ – ½ c water, depending on the consistency of the dough (some granolas are drier than others)

Add all the ingredients to the machine in the order listed. Choose either regular or light crust (depending on your preference) and push "Start."

Third Bread*

So-called because you use two flours and one meal, this unusual bread comes from a traditional pioneer-days' recipe. Expect it to sink a little and to be dense and chewy.

2 t or ½ package of yeast
1½ c bread flour
½ c medium rye flour
½ c cornmeal (yellow or blue)
⅓ c honey
1 t salt
1 c water

Add all the ingredients to the machine in the order listed. Choose either regular or light crust (depending on your preference) and push "Start."

* This recipe is dairy-free.

T This bread may be prepared on the timer; if you use the timer method, though, use active dry yeast (rather than compressed) and if you have a yeast dispenser, use it!

Herb and Spice Breads

These breads are nice to prepare and serve with cheese and crudités for company. Sliced thinly, many are also good as a base for canapés.

Onion Dill Bread

This is a delicious "eat it hot out of the bread machine" bread. It doesn't even need butter. I have had success substituting yogurt for the sour cream for a lower-calorie treat.

- 2 t or 1/2 package of yeast
- 2 c bread flour
- 1/4 t baking soda
- 1 t salt
- 1 egg
- 1/4 c water
- 1/2 c cottage cheese
- 1/2 c sour cream
- 2 T sugar
- 2 T minced dried onion
- 1 T + 1 t dried dill seed
- 1 T butter

In a warm saucepan, combine water, cottage cheese, sour cream, sugar, onion, dill and butter, until melted.

Add all the ingredients to the machine in the order listed. Choose either regular or light crust (depending on your preference) and push "Start."

Mint and Yogurt Bread

This has a rather unusual flavor, not sweet, but very delicate. Spread a thin layer of cream cheese between two thin slices of Mint and Yogurt Bread for a delicious canapé.

2 t or ½ package of yeast
2 c bread flour
¾ c plain yogurt
2 T chopped fresh mint
2 t grated lemon rind
1 t butter
¼ c water

Add all the ingredients to the machine in the order listed. Choose either regular or light crust (depending on your preference) and push "Start."

Dill Bread

This bread is terrific served with fish, particularly swordfish. Try it also for tuna salad sandwiches.

2 t or ½ package of yeast
2½ c bread flour
¼ t baking soda
1 T dill weed
2 T sugar
1 t salt
2 eggs
1 c cottage cheese
½ c water

Add all the ingredients to the machine in the order listed. Choose either regular or light crust (depending on your preference) and push "Start."

R These recipes will work on a "rapid" or "quick bread" setting.

Italian Spice Bread*

This is really excellent toasted or broiled with garlic and butter. Serve it as a snack or with an Italian tomato dish. I served it with lasagne one Christmas Eve and my guests just raved about it.

- 2 t or 1/2 package of yeast
- 2 c bread flour
- 1 t sugar
- 1 t salt
- 2 t each: dried oregano, basil, marjoram
- 3 cloves garlic, minced
- 7/8 c water

Add all the ingredients to the machine in the order listed. Choose either regular or light crust (depending on your preference) and push "Start."

* This recipe is dairy-free.

R This recipe will work on a "rapid" or "quick bread" setting.

T This bread may be prepared on the timer; if you use the timer method, though, use active dry yeast (rather than compressed) and if you have a yeast dispenser, use it!

Garlic and Butter Bread*

You can brush the slices of this bread lightly with olive oil and then broil them as a delicious accompaniment to spaghetti or Pasta Alfredo.

2 t or 1/2 package of yeast
2 c bread flour
2/3 t sugar
3/4 t salt
5 cloves garlic, minced
1/4 c (1/2 stick) margarine (or butter)
2/3 c water

Add all the ingredients to the machine in the order listed. Choose either regular or light crust (depending on your preference) and push "Start."

* This recipe is dairy-free.

R This recipe will work on a "rapid" or "quick bread" setting.

T This bread may be prepared on the timer; if you use the timer method, though, use active dry yeast (rather than compressed) and if you have a yeast dispenser, use it!

Spiced Pepper Bread

This is a very flavorful, unusual bread that is absolutely delicious with a highly spiced soup, such as gazpacho.

- 2 t or ½ package of yeast
- 2 c bread flour
- 3 T sugar
- ½ t salt
- 3 T nonfat dry milk powder
- ½ t ground black pepper
- ½ t anise seed
- ¼ t allspice
- 3 T butter
- 1 egg
- 2 T honey
- 1 T corn syrup
- ¼ c chopped walnuts
- ¾ c water

Add all the ingredients to the machine in the order listed. Choose either regular or light crust (depending on your preference) and push "Start."

Note: Add the walnuts at the beginning if you want them thoroughly mixed in, or at the end of the first kneading or after indicator beep if you would like them more whole.

Vegetable Breads

Vegetable breads are good to serve with soups and stews. They also make good sandwich breads, as well as snacks.

Green Spinach Bread*

The spinach in this bread makes it very rich in iron. Try making toasted cheese sandwiches with it (you may even get the kids to eat their spinach that way!).

2 t or ½ package of yeast
2 c bread flour
½ c medium rye flour
1¼ t salt
¼ t ginger
¼ t sugar
1 t caraway seeds
1 t fennel seeds
1 t dill seeds
1 egg, unbeaten
2 T light vegetable oil
1 package (10 oz) frozen chopped spinach, defrosted but not drained and removed from package
½ c water

Add all the ingredients to the machine in the order listed. Choose either regular or light crust (depending on your preference) and push "Start."

* This recipe is dairy-free.

Potato Bread

Serve this bread with soups or stews—wonderful!

2 t or ½ package of yeast
2 c bread flour
1 T sugar
1 t salt
2 T butter
⅓ c mashed white potatoes
½ – ¾ c milk, depending on how dry or wet your mashed potatoes are (watch the dough and add as necessary)

Follow standard directions, below.

Bloody Mary Bread*

For an open-face sandwich, top slices of bread with sharp cheddar cheese and broil until hot and bubbly.

2 t or ½ package of yeast
2 c bread flour
1 t salt
1 T sugar
1 T soft magarine (or butter)
1 can (6 oz) spicy vegetable juice
1 T vodka
1 egg (optional)

Add all the ingredients to the machine in the order listed. Choose either regular or light crust (depending on your preference) and push "Start."

* This recipe is dairy-free.

Pumpkin Bread*

You can use your leftover pumpkin pie to make a sweet pumpkin bread. For an easier adaptation, you can open and scoop out canned pumpkin. Either way, it's delicious and warming for crisp fall and winter nights.

- 2 t or 1/2 package of yeast
- 2 c bread flour
- 1/2 c wheat flour
- 1 T + 2 t margarine (or butter)
- 1 egg (optional)
- 1/2 c warm water
- 1/4 c orange juice
- 1/2 c pumpkin
- 1 t salt
- 1/2 t cinnamon
- 1/2 t ginger
- 1/2 t grated orange rind

Add all the ingredients to the machine in the order listed. Choose either regular or light crust (depending on your preference) and push "Start."

* This recipe is dairy-free.

Carrot Bread

Here's an easy and delicious way to get your vitamin A. Serve this bread warm with butter and even a touch of cinnamon sugar.

- 3 t or 1 package of yeast
- 1 1/2 c bread flour
- 1/2 c whole wheat flour
- 1 c quick oats
- 3 T nonfat dry milk powder
- 1 T + 2 t brown sugar
- 1 t salt
- 1/2 c grated carrot
- 1 T light vegetable oil
- 3/4 c water

Add all the ingredients to the machine in the order listed. Choose either regular or light crust (depending on your preference) and push "Start."

Winter Squash Bread

You can make this with pumpkin, acorn, or butternut squash.

- 2 t or 1/2 package of yeast
- 2 c bread flour
- 1/2 c 100% whole wheat flour
- 1/4 t ground cloves
- 1/4 t nutmeg
- 1/4 t allspice
- 1 t cinnamon
- 2 T honey
- 1 t salt
- 2 T margarine (or butter)
- 2/3 c cooked and mashed winter squash on bottom
- 1/2 – 3/4 c milk, depending on how dry or wet your squash is (watch the dough and add as necessary)

Add all the ingredients to the machine in the order listed. Choose either regular or light crust (depending on your preference) and push "Start."

Note: you can substitute canned pumpkin for the squash. Simply open the can and scoop out 2/3 cup.

Sweet Potato Bread

This is a great way to use leftover sweet potatoes after Thanksgiving dinner.

2 t or ½ package of yeast
2 c bread flour
2 T brown sugar
⅔ t salt
2 T butter
⅓ c cooked and mashed sweet potatoes
½ c water

Add all the ingredients to the machine in the order listed. Choose either regular or light crust (depending on your preference) and push "Start."

Zucchini Wheat Bread*

This is perfect with winter soups and thick bisques. Try it toasted with butter.

2 t or ½ package of yeast
1 c bread flour
1 c 100% whole wheat flour
2 T wheat germ
1 t grated orange rind
2 T honey
1 t salt
2 T margarine (or butter)
½ c shredded zucchini
¾ c water

Add all the ingredients to the machine in the order listed. Choose either regular or light crust (depending on your preference) and push "Start."

* This recipe is dairy-free.

Onion Bread

Great for hamburgers and barbeque dinners!

2 t or ½ package of yeast
2 c bread flour
1 T nonfat dry milk
powder
1 T sugar
1 t salt
¾ c grated onion
1 T + 1 t butter
⅞ c water

Add all the ingredients to the machine in the order listed. Choose either regular or light crust (depending on your preference) and push "Start."

California Dip Bread

Onion soup mix is the miracle ingredient in this recipe. This bread will be gone almost as soon as you put it out, so if you're planning on serving it at a party, make several loaves!

2 t or ½ package of yeast
2 c bread flour
⅛ t baking soda
2 T sugar
1 egg
½ c cottage cheese
½ c sour cream
1 T butter
3 T water
1 envelope onion soup
mix (or to taste)

Add all the ingredients to the machine in the order listed. Choose either regular or light crust (depending on your preference) and push "Start."

Chili, Corn and Cheese Bread

Serve this with a Mexican meal or Gazpacho soup. Add the liquid slowly when you make this recipe. If the corn and chilis aren't drained thoroughly you might end up with dough that's too soupy. If this happens, add flour a small bit at a time.

(Follow standard directions below.)

2 t or 1/2 package of yeast
2 c bread flour
1/2 c cornmeal
1/3 c drained corn niblets, frozen or canned
2 t chopped, canned chilies
1/2 c shredded sharp cheddar or Jack
1 egg
1 T butter
1 t sugar
1/2 t salt
1 c water

Walnut and Red Onion Bread

Serve this with soup, or as a very unusual hamburger bun. Sweet white onions are also marvelous in this bread.

2 t or 1/2 package of yeast
2 c bread flour
1 t sugar
1 t salt
3 T butter
1/3 c chopped red onion
1/2 c chopped walnuts
7/8 c milk

Add all the ingredients to the machine in the order listed. Choose either regular or light crust (depending on your preference) and push "Start."

Sourdough Breads

Slightly sour and often quite tangy, sourdough breads are good for absolutely everything, especially turkey and chicken sandwiches and as a topping for French onion soup.

Sourdough Starter

Don't be intimidated by the prospect of making sourdough starter. It's not nearly as difficult as people tend to think. And once you have the starter established, it's as easy as can be to maintain.

3 t or 1 package of yeast

2 c lukewarm milk, whole or low fat

2 c bread flour

1. Combine all ingredients in a bowl and mix well with a hand mixer.

2. Pour the starter mixture into a large bowl or jar which you can seal tightly and leave alone. (I use a large honey pot.)

3. The first time you make the starter, allow it to sit for a week at room temperature. Stir or shake the mixture once a day.

4. The starter is now ready to use in your bread recipes. Every time you take a cup out to make bread, you must "feed" the starter by adding an additional cup each of flour and either milk or water (alternate each time). Let the "fed" starter sit at room temperature for one full day, then store it in the refrigerator until the next time you are ready to use it. (At that time, you'll repeat the "feeding" process: use it, feed it, leave it out for one full day, and return it to the refrigerator.)

Starter Strategies

- If your starter changes color, throw it out.
- If your starter develops a foul odor, throw it out.

- You must use the starter and re-feed it *at least* once a week. If you don't feel like making bread, simply discard a cup of starter and add a cup each of flour and liquid.
- While the starter is being stored in the refrigerator, stir or shake it every few days.
- Starter may be frozen for up to a month, then gently thawed in the refrigerator.
- Treated properly, starter lasts forever.

San Francisco Sourdough

This is my favorite bread for turkey sandwiches with lettuce, tomato and mayonnaise! It's also terrific for BLT's.

2 t or ½ package of yeast
2 c bread flour
1 T sugar
2 t salt
2 T butter
½ c milk
1 c sourdough starter

Add all the ingredients to the machine in the order listed. Choose either regular or light crust (depending on your preference) and push "Start."

Sourdough Wheat Bread

A slightly denser sandwich bread, this is also excellent with soups.

2 t or ½ package of yeast	1 T salt
1 c bread flour	2 T butter
1 c whole wheat flour	⅔ c milk
2 T sugar	1 c starter

Add all the ingredients to the machine in the order listed. Choose either regular or light crust (depending on your preference) and push "Start."

Sourdough French Bread

I like this with Swiss cheese fondue, but it's also very, very good simply toasted and buttered.

2 t or ½ package of yeast	1 t salt
2 c bread flour	⅔ c water
2 t sugar	1 c starter

Add all the ingredients to the machine in the order listed. Choose either regular or light crust (depending on your preference) and push "Start."

Rye Breads

Rye is the bread of choice for deli sandwiches—its tangy flavor is excellent with cured meats and mustards.

New York Deli Rye

This is my favorite rye, perfect for pastrami or corned beef sandwiches.

2 t or 1/2 package yeast
3/4 c medium rye flour
1 1/2 c bread flour
3 T nonfat dry milk powder
2 t caraway seeds, optional
1 T + 1 t honey
3/4 t salt
1 T light vegetable oil
7/8 c water

Add all the ingredients to the machine in the order listed. Choose either regular or light crust (depending on your preference) and push "Start."

Orange and Rye Beer Bread

This is another great sandwich rye, but it's also good served plain with chunks of sharp cheese.

- 2 t or ½ package of yeast
- ¾ c medium rye flour
- 1¾ c bread flour
- 2 T wheat germ
- 1 t salt
- 2 T molasses
- 2 t grated orange rind
- 2 T butter
- 1 c warm beer

Add all the ingredients to the machine in the order listed. Choose either regular or light crust (depending on your preference) and push "Start."

Orange and Rye Bread

A bit less tangy than orange and rye beer bread, this is suitable for mild meat sandwiches, like chicken and turkey.

- 2 t or ½ package yeast
- 1½ c bread flour
- 1 c rye flour
- ¼ c honey
- 1½ t salt
- 1 T butter
- 2 t caraway seeds, optional
- ½ t orange peel
- 1 c water

Add all the ingredients to the machine in the order listed. Choose either regular or light crust (depending on your preference) and push "Start."

Whole Wheat Rye Bread

For those who like a very hearty, dense sandwich bread, this is ideal.

- 2 t or 1/2 package of yeast
- 1 1/4 c bread flour
- 3/4 c rye flour
- 1/4 c whole wheat flour
- 2 t caraway seeds
- 1/3 c molasses
- 1/2 t salt
- 2 T butter
- 3/4 c water

Add all the ingredients to the machine in the order listed. Choose either regular or light crust (depending on your preference) and push "Start."

Pumpernickel Breads

"You shall find out how salt is the taste of another man's bread, and how hard is the way up and down another man's stairs."

Dante, Paradiso

Light Pumpernickel Bread*

This is a good bread for all sorts of deli sandwiches.

2 t or 1/2 package of yeast
1 c bread flour
1 c rye flour
2 T cocoa powder
2 t caraway seeds
1 T sugar
1 t salt
2 T molasses
1 T light vegetable oil
3/4 c water

Add all the ingredients to the machine in the order listed. Choose either regular or light crust (depending on your preference) and push "Start."

* This recipe is dairy-free.

Dark Pumpernickel Bread*

This rich, dark pumpernickel is perfect with hearty stews.

2 t or 1/2 package yeast
1 c bread flour
3/4 c whole wheat flour
3/4 c rye flour
2 t caraway seeds
1 t instant coffee powder
1 T + 1 t cocoa powder
1 T brown sugar
2 T molasses
1 t salt
2 T light vegetable oil
3/4 c water

Add all the ingredients to the machine in the order listed. Choose either regular or light crust (depending on your preference) and push "Start."

* This recipe is dairy-free.

Fruit Breads

Fruit breads make lovely snacks and tea breads. They are particularly nice sliced and quartered, then served as finger food at parties.

Fruit Cocktail Bread*

This is akin to fruitcake—only much, much better. Serve it in place of fruitcake at your holiday spread.

- 2 t or 1/2 package of yeast
- 2 c bread flour
- 1/2 t ginger
- 1/4 t nutmeg
- 1/2 c chopped macadamia nuts (or pecans)
- 1 T grated orange rind
- 1 T honey
- 1 t salt
- 1 T margarine (or butter)
- 1 (15 oz) can fruit cocktail, drained
- 1/2 c water

Add all the ingredients to the machine in the order listed. Choose either regular or light crust (depending on your preference) and push "Start."

* This recipe is dairy-free.

R This recipe will work on a "rapid" or "quick bread" setting.

T This bread may be prepared on the timer; if you use the timer method, though, use active dry yeast (rather than compressed) and if you have a yeast dispenser, use it!

Banana Wheat Bread*

You may use an extra banana or two in this recipe—it becomes more moist and dense the more you add. Rich in potassium, this is a very nutritious snack.

2 t or 1/2 package of yeast
1 c bread flour
1 c wheat flour
1/2 t salt
1 t poppy seeds
2 small ripe bananas, sliced

1/4 c honey
1 egg (optional)
2 T light vegetable oil
1/2 t vanilla
1/4 c water

Add all the ingredients to the machine in the order listed. Choose either regular or light crust (depending on your preference) and push "Start."

* This recipe is dairy-free.

Orange Bread*

This tangy sweet bread is perfect for holiday buffets.

2 t or 1/2 package of yeast
2 c bread flour
3 T sugar
1 t salt
1 T margarine (or butter)

1 egg (optional)
2 T grated orange rind
1/2 c + 2 T orange juice
2 T water

Add all the ingredients to the machine in the order listed. Choose either regular or light crust (depending on your preference) and push "Start."

* This recipe is dairy-free.

R This recipe will work on a "rapid" or "quick bread" setting.

T This bread may be prepared on the timer; if you use the timer method, though, use active dry yeast (rather than compressed) and if you have a yeast dispenser, use it!

Applesauce Bread*

This makes a nice breakfast bread. Children and adults love it toasted with a little bit of butter and cinnamon sugar sprinkled on top.

- 2 t or ½ package of yeast
- 2 c bread flour
- ½ t salt
- 4 T sugar
- 1 t cinnamon
- pinch nutmeg
- ½ c applesauce, mildly sweetened
- 1 T margarine (or butter)
- ½ c apple juice
- ½ c grated apple
- ¼ c raisins (optional)

Add all the ingredients to the machine in the order listed. Choose either regular or light crust (depending on your preference) and push "Start."

* This recipe is dairy-free.

Apple Pie Bread*

Serve this with vanilla ice cream!

- 2 t or ½ package of yeast
- 2 c bread flour
- ¼ c sugar
- 1 t salt
- 2 t cinnamon
- ⅞ c margarine (or butter)
- 1 c peeled, cored and sliced apples (I like Granny Smith)

Put ingredients into the bread pan in the order listed. Bake on full bake cycle.

Add the apples after the first kneading or at the indicator.

* This recipe is dairy-free.

R This recipe will work on a "rapid" or "quick bread" setting.

Peach Bread*

They say that the test of a truly great bread is whether it can stand on its own, without embellishments. I submit this peach bread for your consideration. . . .

- 2 t or ½ package of yeast
- 2 c bread flour
- ½ t salt
- 4 T sugar
- ½ t cinnamon
- pinch nutmeg
- ⅔ c applesauce, mildly sweetened
- 1 T margarine (or butter)
- ¼ – ½ c apple juice, depending on how juicy the peach and applesauce are
- ½ c grated peach (or pear)

Add all the ingredients to the machine in the order listed. Choose either regular or light crust (depending on your preference) and push "Start."

* This recipe is dairy-free.

R This recipe will work on a "rapid" or "quick bread" setting.

T This bread may be prepared on the timer; if you use the timer method, though, use active dry yeast (rather than compressed) and if you have a yeast dispenser, use it!

Blueberry Bread*

Another great breakfast bread—and a terrific substitute for blueberry muffins at a brunch buffet.

2 t or ½ package of yeast	1 can (16½ oz) blueberries, drained (save the liquid)
2 c bread flour	¼ c blueberry liquid
2 T sugar	½ c water
½ t salt	
1 T margarine (or butter)	

Add all the ingredients to the machine in the order listed. Choose either regular or light crust (depending on your preference) and push "Start."

* This recipe is dairy-free.

R This recipe will work on a "rapid" or "quick bread" setting.

T This bread may be prepared on the timer; if you use the timer method, though, use active dry yeast (rather than compressed) and if you have a yeast dispenser, use it!

Cinnamon Raisin Bread

In order to keep the raisins intact, add them at the end of the first kneading. If you prefer to have the nutritional value of the raisins without the chewiness, add them at the beginning with the rest of the ingredients.

2 t or ½ package of yeast	2 t cinnamon
2 c bread flour	1 T butter
2 T sugar	⅞ c milk
1 t salt	⅔ c raisins (optional)

Add all the ingredients to the machine in the order listed. Choose either regular or light crust (depending on your preference) and push "Start."

R This recipe will work on a "rapid" or "quick bread" setting.

T This bread may be prepared on the timer; if you use the timer method, though, use active dry yeast (rather than compressed) and if you have a yeast dispenser, use it!

Sweet Lemon Bread

You may replace the lemon with lime in this recipe. Serve with a Mexican meal or with Margaritas after dinner.

2 t or ½ package of yeast
2 c bread flour
¼ c sugar
½ t salt
¼ c (½ stick) butter
1 egg plus 1 egg yolk
¼ t lemon extract
2 t grated lemon rind
¾ c milk, scalded

Add all the ingredients to the machine in the order listed. Choose either regular or light crust (depending on your preference) and push "Start."

Apricot Bread*

You may use any dried fruit for this bread, or even a handful of mixed ones. (I've used apple, with apple juice rather than orange juice, with delicious results.)

3 t or 1 package of yeast
2 c bread flour
2 T sugar
⅔ t salt
2 T margarine (or butter)
¾ c orange juice
½ c dried apricots

Add all the ingredients to the machine in the order listed. Choose either regular or light crust (depending on your preference) and push "Start."

* This recipe is dairy-free.

R This recipe will work on a "rapid" or "quick bread" setting.

T This bread may be prepared on the timer; if you use the timer method, though, use active dry yeast (rather than compressed) and if you have a yeast dispenser, use it!

Strawberry Banana Bread*

Take advantage of berry season with this fruity bread.

2 t or 1/2 package of yeast
2 c bread flour
1/2 t salt
2 small ripe bananas, sliced
3/4 c sliced strawberries
1/4 c honey
1 egg (optional)
2 T margarine (or butter)
1/2 t vanilla
1/2 c water

Add all the ingredients to the machine in the order listed. Choose either regular or light crust (depending on your preference) and push "Start."

* This recipe is dairy-free.

R This recipe will work on a "rapid" or "quick bread" setting.

T This bread may be prepared on the timer; if you use the timer method, though, use active dry yeast (rather than compressed) and if you have a yeast dispenser, use it!

Apple Butter Bread*

The whole wheat flour and low sugar content of this bread make it an extra-nutritious autumn breakfast bread. Spread generously with apple butter.

2 t or ½ package of yeast
1½ c bread flour
1 c whole wheat flour
1 T sugar
1 t salt
¾ c apple butter
2 T margarine (or butter)
1 egg (optional)
¼ c water, more if necessary (This depends on the liquid content of the apple butter you use, just check the dough while it's kneading. It should be smooth and elastic, just a little sticky to the touch.)

Add all the ingredients to the machine in the order listed. Choose either regular or light crust (depending on your preference) and push "Start."

* This recipe is dairy-free.

R This recipe will work on a "rapid" or "quick bread" setting.

Banana Oat Bread*

Oatmeal lovers will delight in the moist texture and sweet banana taste of this bread. Sprinkle loose oats on top just before baking for the scrumptious look of toasted oatmeal.

2 t or ½ package of yeast
2 c bread flour
1 c quick or rolled oats
1 T sugar
1 t salt
2 T light vegetable oil
1 egg (optional)
2 medium size, ripe bananas mashed
1 c water

Add all the ingredients to the machine in the order listed. Choose either regular or light crust (depending on your preference) and push "Start."

* This recipe is dairy-free.

R This recipe will work on a "rapid" or "quick bread" setting.

Piña Colada Bread

Great with piña coladas! Serve this bread with a Polynesian dinner or as a summer snack.

- 2 t or 1/2 package of yeast
- 2 c bread flour
- 3 T sugar
- 1/2 t salt
- 1/4–1/2 c grated coconut (to taste)
- 3 T butter
- 2 t pineapple extract
- 1 (8 oz) can of crushed pineapple, drained
- 2/3 c cream cheese
- 1/2 c coconut milk

Add all the ingredients to the machine in the order listed. Choose either regular or light crust (depending on your preference) and push "Start."

R This recipe will work on a "rapid" or "quick bread" setting.

Traditional Raisin Bread*

A lightly sweet bread great for toasting, or smothering with peanut butter and jelly.

3 t or 1 package of yeast
2 c bread flour
2 T sugar
2/3 t salt
3 T margarine (or butter)
1/2 c raisins or currants
3/4 c water

Add all the ingredients to the machine in the order listed. Choose either regular or light crust (depending on your preference) and push "Start."

Note: You may add the raisins at the beginning and they will be well blended into the bread. This is what you will have with the timer. If you prefer the raisins whole, add them at the end of the first kneading, or at the indicator.

* This recipe is dairy-free.

R This recipe will work on a "rapid" or "quick bread" setting.

T This bread may be prepared on the timer; if you use the timer method, though, use active dry yeast (rather than compressed) and if you have a yeast dispenser, use it!

Raisin Nut Bread

This is a very sweet bread, loaded with iron from the raisins and currants and protein from the nuts. This bread has a very liquidy dough—don't worry, it will bake firm and tender.

- 2 t or ½ package of yeast
- 2 c bread flour
- 3 T sugar
- 1 t salt
- 1 egg
- 4 T butter
- 3 T honey
- ¼ c raisins
- ¼ c currants
- ½ c chopped mixed nuts
- ½ c milk
- ½ c water

Follow standard directions, below.
Note: Add the raisins, currants and nuts at the beginning of the cycle for well-blended bread, or at the end of the first kneading for chunkier bread.

Prune Bread*

This is similar to prune Danish, only much less fattening.

- 2 t or ½ package of yeast
- 2 c bread flour
- 2 T + 2 t brown sugar
- ¾ t salt
- 1 T margarine (or butter)
- ¾ c prunes, pitted and quartered
- ⅞ c water

Add all the ingredients to the machine in the order listed. Choose either regular or light crust (depending on your preference) and push "Start."

* This recipe is dairy-free.

R This recipe will work on a "rapid" or "quick bread" setting.

T This bread may be prepared on the timer; if you use the timer method, though, use active dry yeast (rather than compressed) and if you have a yeast dispenser, use it!

Dessert Breads

These breads are perfect with coffee or hot chocolate after dinner, or with afternoon tea. They also are good served at buffets and cocktail parties.

Sweet Bread

This sweet bread is nice at teatime, spread with jelly and butter.

- 2 t or ½ package of yeast
- 2 c bread flour
- 3 T sugar
- ½ t salt
- 2 T butter
- 1 egg
- ⅞ c milk

Add all the ingredients to the machine in the order listed. Choose either regular or light crust (depending on your preference) and push "Start."

Colonial Sweet Bread*

Cornmeal and molasses were much used in early American cooking. This recipe makes the same bread enjoyed as a staple food by our founding fathers.

- 2 t or ½ package of yeast
- 2 c bread flour
- ¼ c cornmeal
- 3 T molasses
- ½ t salt
- 1 T margarine (or butter)
- 1 c water

Add all the ingredients to the machine in the order listed. Choose either regular or light crust (depending on your preference) and push "Start."

* This recipe is dairy-free.

R This recipe will work on a "rapid" or "quick bread" setting.

T This bread may be prepared on the timer; if you use the timer method, though, use active dry yeast (rather than compressed) and if you have a yeast dispenser, use it!

Peanut Butter Bread*

This is really a nice snack bread, but it's also terrific to send in lunchboxes for a new twist on the standard peanut butter and jelly sandwich.

- 2 t or ½ package of yeast
- 2 c bread flour
- 3 T brown sugar, packed
- ⅓ c chunky peanut butter
- 1 c water

Add all the ingredients to the machine in the order listed. Choose either regular or light crust (depending on your preference) and push "Start."

Tip: To measure and add the peanut butter put some oil in the measuring cup first, swirl it around, and pour it out. The peanut butter will then measure easily and slide right out.

* This recipe is dairy-free.

R This recipe will work on a "rapid" or "quick bread" setting.

T This bread may be prepared on the timer; if you use the timer method, though, use active dry yeast (rather than compressed) and if you have a yeast dispenser, use it!

Peanut Butter and Jelly Bread*

This is the favorite recipe of several of my little friends. What they don't know is that it's high in protein and healthy for them. What they do know is that it's delicious.

2 t or ½ package of yeast
2 c bread flour
3 T brown sugar, packed
⅓ c low-sugar chunky peanut butter
3 T no-sugar-added fruit preserves
1 c water

Add all the ingredients to the machine in the order listed. Choose either regular or light crust (depending on your preference) and push "Start."

* This recipe is dairy-free.

T This bread may be prepared on the timer; if you use the timer method, though, use active dry yeast (rather than compressed) and if you have a yeast dispenser, use it!

Chunky Peanut Bread

This is a great bread for active kids—and adults. The peanuts provide protein and energy, but be aware that this delicious bread contains peanuts and is therefore quite fattening.

2 t or ½ package of yeast
1½ c bread flour
½ c whole wheat flour
3 T nonfat dry milk powder
2 T sugar
2 T butter
1 egg
½ c chopped salted peanuts
¾ c water

Add all the ingredients to the machine in the order listed. Choose either regular or light crust (depending on your preference) and push "Start."

T This bread may be prepared on the timer; if you use the timer method, though, use active dry yeast (rather than compressed) and if you have a yeast dispenser, use it!

Chocolate Bread

Chocolate lovers rejoice! This has much less fat than chocolate cake and satisfies even the most desperate chocolate craving. This is the trickiest loaf in the book to get right. Make sure you keep an eye on the dough as it's kneading—it should be elastic but just a little stickier than most. If the loaf is too stiff, it won't rise properly. Also, keep in mind that this makes a dense loaf, not a light, fluffy one.

3 t or 1 package of yeast
2 c bread flour
1 c sugar
½ c cocoa powder
2 eggs
1 t vanilla extract
3 T butter
1 c milk

Follow standard directions, below.

Chocolate Chip Bread

Almost more cake than bread, this is a nice addition to buffets and holiday spreads. You may add the chocolate chips at the beginning of the cycle so they will be finely blended, or wait until after the first kneading so that they appear more visible.

2 t or ½ package yeast
2 c bread flour
2 T brown sugar
1 T white sugar
1 t salt
1 t cinnamon
2 T soft butter
1 egg
1 c milk
1 c semi-sweet chocolate chips

Add all the ingredients to the machine in the order listed. Choose either regular or light crust (depending on your preference) and push "Start."

R This recipe will work on a "rapid" or "quick bread" setting.

Holiday Breads

Throughout the holiday seasons, from Thanksgiving and Christmas right through New Year's, you'll find favorites in these pages that you'll go back to year after year.

Vortlimpa (Swedish Holiday Rye)

This wonderful bread comes out moist and slightly sweet. Because of its full, satisfying flavor it is quite nice eaten alone, as well as used for sandwiches. I always make extra so that there is enough to make sandwiches later with the leftover holiday ham and turkey.

2 t or ½ package of yeast
2 c rye flour
1 c bread flour
1 T ground fennel seeds
2 t grated orange peel
1 t salt
⅓ c molasses
3 T butter
1 c room temperature dark beer or stout

Put the ingredients into the bread machine in the order listed, set the machine to a regular bake cycle, and push "Start."

R This recipe will work on a "rapid" or "quick bread" setting.

Moravian Christmas Bread

This subtle fruit bread makes an excellent gift. As it bakes, the scent is just heavenly, so it's a wonderful bread to serve on the day of a holiday party.

BATTER:

- 2 t or 1/2 package of yeast
- 2 1/2 c flour
- 1 c milk, scalded and cooled to warm
- 1/3 c melted butter
- 1/4 c sugar
- 1/2 t salt
- 1/3 c currants, scalded, drained and dried
- 3 T chopped candied pineapple
- 3 T chopped candied lemon rind
- 3 T chopped candied orange rind

GLAZE:

- 1 egg beaten with 1 T water

Combine all the bread ingredients in the pan of your bread machine and bake on the full bake cycle. As soon as the bread is done, remove it from the pan, brush the glaze on it, and put it back into the pan to set the glaze for several minutes in the still-warm machine.

Vanoce (Bohemian Christmas Bread)

This recipe was given to me by a friend who recommends that it be served warm with coffee after dinner on Christmas Eve.

BATTER:

- 3 t or 1 package of yeast
- 3 c flour
- 3 T water
- ⅓ c sugar
- ¼ t ginger
- ¼ t mace
- 1 T grated lemon rind
- ¼ c heavy cream
- ½ c milk
- 3 T butter, melted
- 1 t salt
- 1 egg
- ¾ c raisins, scalded and drained
- ¼ c chopped almonds

GLAZE:

- 1 egg yolk mixed with 1 T water
- sliced almonds

Combine all the ingredients except for the raisins and almonds in the pan of your bread machine and set it for a full cycle.

Add the raisins and almonds at the indicator beep or during the second knead.

When the bread is done, remove it from the pan and brush on the glaze. Top with sliced almonds. Quickly return it to the pan and then to the still-warm bread machine for a few minutes to set.

Vanocka (Czechoslovakian Christmas Bread)

This variation of the Bohemian Vanoce calls for both butter and lard, though you may use all butter or, if you prefer, a mixture of butter and vegetable shortening.

BATTER:

- 3 t or 1 package of yeast
- 2 c flour
- 1/3 c sugar
- 1 t salt
- 1/4 c water
- 1/4 c evaporated milk
- 3 T butter, softened
- 3 T lard
- 1 egg
- 1 egg yolk
- 1 t lemon zest
- 1/2 t vanilla extract
- 1/4 c raisins
- 1/4 c sliced almonds

GLAZE:

- 1 egg yolk mixed with 1 T water
- sliced almonds

Put the ingredients into the bread machine in the order listed, set the machine to a regular bake cycle, and push "Start."

When the bread is done, remove it from the pan and brush on the glaze. Top with sliced almonds. Quickly return it to the pan and then to the still-warm bread machine for a few minutes to set.

Greek Holiday Bread

This has a rather unusual flavor, not sweet, but very delicate.

- 2 t or 1/2 package of yeast
- 2 c bread flour
- 3/4 c plain yogurt
- 1/2 c sugar
- 2 T chopped fresh mint
- 2 t grated lemon rind
- 1/4 t lemon extract
- 1 t butter
- 1/2 c water

Add all the ingredients to the machine in the order listed. Choose either regular or light crust (depending on your preference) and push "Start."

Egg Nog Bread

This is one of the most tender loaves I've ever eaten and it's almost impossible not to devour it as soon as it comes out of the machine. If you don't have egg nog, you may use milk. But be warned: this is an unusually sticky dough and you needn't add more flour to it.

- 2 t or 1/2 package of yeast
- 2 c flour
- 1 T dark corn syrup
- 1 t salt
- 3 eggs
- 1 c egg nog (non-alcohol)

Put the ingredients into the bread machine in the order listed, set the machine to a regular bake cycle, and push "Start."

R This recipe will work on a "rapid" or "quick bread" setting.

T This bread may be prepared on the timer.

Scottish Black Bread

This is another nice holiday bread, particularly as a more savory alternative to fruitcake.

3 t or 1 package
2 c flour
3/4 c water
1 T sugar
2 T nonfat dry milk powder
1 t salt
1/4 c (or 1/2 stick) butter
1 egg
2 T brandy
4 T grated orange rind
1 c currants
1 c raisins

Put the ingredients into the bread machine in the order listed, select the full bake cycle, and push "Start."

Norwegian Sweet Bread

In Norway there are two traditional holiday breads: this sweet bread and another "Christmas Bread" where the bread is decorated with candies. I make both during the holidays because some people prefer a plain cake-like treat to the embellished version.

2 t or 1/2 package of yeast
2 1/2 c bread flour
1 c milk
1/4 c melted butter
1/4 c sugar
2 eggs, lightly beaten
1 t salt

Put the ingredients into the bread machine in the order listed, set the machine to a regular bake cycle, and push "Start."

R This recipe will work on a "rapid" or "quick bread" setting.

Jule Kake
(Norwegian Christmas Bread)

Jule Kake begins with a base of Norwegian Sweet Bread that becomes quite sweet and dessert-like with the addition of candied fruit.

BATTER:

- 2 t or 1/2 package of yeast
- 2 1/2 c bread flour
- 1 c milk
- 1/4 c melted butter
- 1/4 c sugar
- 1/4 t cardamom
- 1 t salt
- 2 eggs, lightly beaten
- 1/4 c candied cherries
- 1/4 c candied mixed fruit
- 1/4 c currants

GLAZE:

- 1 egg beaten with 1 T water
- Sliced almonds

Put the ingredients, except the candied fruit and currants, into the bread machine and bake on a regular cycle.

Add the candied fruit and currants after the first kneading.

When the bread is done, remove it from the pan and brush on the glaze. Top with sliced almonds. Quickly return it to the pan and then to the still-warm bread machine for a few minutes to set.

Poteca (Yugoslavian Christmas Bread)

This heavenly bread must be prepared on the "dough" cycle, then rolled out, filled with the walnut filling, and baked in a conventional oven.

BATTER:

- 2 t or ½ package of yeast
- 3 c bread flour
- ½ c sour cream
- 2 T milk
- 2 T water
- ¼ c butter (½ stick)
- ⅓ c sugar
- 2 egg yolks (save the whites)
- ¼ t salt

FILLING

- ½ lb shelled walnuts
- 2 egg whites
- ½ c sugar
- 1 t grated lemon rind

Combine all the ingredients in the bread machine and set it for the "dough" cycle. Prepare the walnut filling in a blender or food processor, by chopping the walnuts to a very fine crumb. Beat the egg whites to stiff and beat in the sugar. Fold the walnuts and lemon rind in gently.

When the dough is ready, remove it from the bread machine and roll it out to a 25″ × 10″ rectangle. Spread the walnut filling on top of the dough and roll it up, jellyroll style.

Put the dough, seam side down, on a 10″ greased tube pan. Cover with a cloth and let rise for 20 minutes.

Heat the oven to 350 degrees.

Bake the Poteca for 40 minutes to a golden brown.

Panettone Di Natale (Italian Sweet Bread)

This classic Italian Christmas bread is very sweet and should be served as a coffee cake or dessert. Since it is traditionally baked in a tall, cylindrical shape, it is perfectly suited for the bread machine.

BATTER

3 t or 1 package of yeast	1/4 c water
2 c bread flour	1/4 t salt
1/3 c milk	2 eggs
1/4 c sugar	1 t grated lemon rind
1/4 c butter (1/2 stick)	1/4 c candied mixed fruits
1/2 t anise seeds	1/4 c raisins

FROSTING:

1 T butter	1 1/2 t heavy cream
1/2 c confectioners sugar	1/4 t almond extract

GARNISH:

whole almonds

citron, julienned

Combine all the ingredients, except for the candied fruit and raisins, in the bread machine and bake on a regular cycle. Add the fruit after the first kneading or at the indicator beep. When the bread is done and slightly cooled, prepare frosting by creaming the butter and sugar together with an electric mixer. Add the cream and almond extract and beat to a creamy consistency. Frost the Panettone when it has cooled. Garnish as desired.

Stollen (German Christmas Bread)

This traditional German bread is filled with candied fruits and topped with a sweet icing. It makes a beautiful holiday gift.

BATTER:

- 3 t or 1 package of yeast
- 3 c flour
- 1/4 c water
- 1/4 c + 2 T milk
- 1/4 c sugar
- 1/2 t salt
- 1/3 c melted butter
- 2 eggs
- 2 t grated lemon rind
- 1/4 c blanched almonds, chopped
- 1/3 c candied mixed fruit, chopped
- 1/4 c raisins, scalded and drained

ICING:

- 1/2 c confectioners sugar
- 1/4 t vanilla
- milk, to make a thick paste

GARNISH:

- sliced candied cherries
- chopped nuts

Combine all batter ingredients except for the fruit and nuts, in the bread machine and set it for the "dough" cycle. Add the fruit and nuts after the first kneading or at the indicator beep.

Grease a baking sheet. When the dough is ready, remove it from the machine and roll it into a 12″ × 8″ oval. Fold it in half, omelet-style, cover and let rise until it's doubled in bulk (45 minutes).

Bake in a 375-degree oven for 30 minutes, or until golden brown. When the stollen has cooled, combine icing ingredients, frost the bread, then garnish it with candied cherry slices and chopped nuts.

Pain d'Epice*
(French Christmas Bread)

This recipe for French Christmas bread was given to me by a friend who wanted me to help her create a bread machine adaptation of it. I'm glad she did, because in the process I discovered a unique savory bread to use throughout the entire holiday season.

2 t or ½ package of yeast
1 c bread flour
1 c rye flour
1 t margarine (or butter)
¾ c water
¼ t salt
½ c honey
1 t anise
1 t + ¼ t allspice
½ t ground ginger

Put the ingredients into the bread machine in the order listed, set the machine to a regular bake cycle, and push "Start."

* This recipe is dairy-free.

Saffron Braid

This braided bread is a traditional Swedish staple. Although the original takes hours, this can be prepared in the bread machine like any other loaf.

- 2 t or ½ package of yeast
- 2 c flour
- ½ c milk
- 2 T water
- ¼ c sugar
- 1 T butter
- ¼ t salt
- pinch of saffron
- 1 egg
- ¼ t cardamom
- 1 egg, beaten
- large-granule sugar

Select the "dough" or "manual" mode on your bread machine. Add ingredients, except egg and granule sugar, in the order listed and push "Start."

When the dough is ready, remove it from the machine and divide it into 3 equal parts. Put them on a cookie sheet and join them all at the very top. Then, very carefully, braid them down to the bottom.

Cover the braid with a dishcloth and let it rise in a warm, draft-free place for 45 minutes.

Brush the egg on the braid then sprinkle the sugar on.

Bake at 375 degrees for 45 minutes, or until the top is lightly browned.

Rosco De Reyes

This traditional Mexican celebration bread is shaped into the form of a ring and served for good luck on New Year's. However, it will also work on the regular full bake cycle in the bread machine without shaping.

BATTER:

- 2 t or ½ package of yeast
- 2½ c bread flour
- ½ c milk
- ¼ c water
- ½ c sugar
- ½ c melted butter
- ½ t salt
- 1 t grated lemon rind
- 3 eggs, beaten
- ¼ c raisins
- ¼ c chopped pecans
- 1 dried pinto bean, wrapped in foil (baked in, to bring luck to the finder)

CONFECTIONERS ICING:

- ¼ c confectioners sugar
- ½ t lemon juice
- water, to make a thick paste

Select the "dough" or "manual" mode on your bread machine. Add all Batter ingredients in the order listed and push "Start."

You may either shape the bread into a ring—foil-wrapped bean, as well—and bake it at 350 degrees for 40 minutes or proceed with the usual bread cycle.

When the bread is done and slightly cooled, mix together icing ingredients and spread the frosting liberally over the top.

Dough Recipes

Even when it can't actually shape and bake certain things, your bread machine does the hard work of kneading, rising, and timing rises and rests for you. All you do is remove the prepared dough, then shape and bake it.

Pizza Dough*

A pizza is only as good as its crust and this crust makes an excellent pizza. If you find it too crispy on the outside, use less olive oil.

3 t or 1 package of yeast (I find compressed far better in this instance)
3 c bread flour
1 T sugar
2 t salt
1 c water
2 T olive oil

Select the "dough" or "manual" mode on your bread machine.

Add ingredients in the order listed and push "Start."

This makes two 9″ pizzas. Freeze them, or top and bake at 475 degrees for 12–15 minutes, or until cheese is melted and bubbly and the crust is lightly browned.

Note: This only needs to sit for one rising.

* This recipe is dairy-free.

Tomato Basil Pizza Dough*

This crust is no mere vehicle for sauce and cheese; it has a wonderful, satisfying flavor in and of itself. Whenever I serve this pizza, my guests ask for the recipe. And it's so tasty that no one ever leaves their crusts on the plate the way they so often do with carryout pizza.

3 t or 1 package of yeast
3 c bread flour
1 c tomato juice
2 T olive oil
1 T sugar
2 t salt
2 T dried chopped basil

Select the "dough" or "manual" mode on your bread machine.

Add ingredients in the order listed and push "Start."

This makes two 9″ pizzas. Freeze them, or top and bake at 475 degrees for 12–15 minutes, or until cheese is melted and bubbly and the crust is lightly browned.

Note: This only needs to sit for one rising.

* This recipe is dairy-free.

Cheese Pizza Dough

The cheese in this crust is really a very pleasant difference. You may even like to sprinkle some on the pizza sheet before you put the dough down.

3 t or 1 package of yeast
3 c bread flour
1 T sugar
2 t salt
½ c grated parmesan cheese
2 T olive oil
1 c water

Select the "dough" or "manual" mode on your bread machine.

Add ingredients in the order listed and push "Start."

This makes two 9″ pizzas. Freeze them, or top and bake at 475 degrees for 12–15 minutes, or until cheese is melted and bubbly and the crust is lightly browned.

Note: This dough only needs one rising.

Sourdough Pizza Dough

This is amazingly delicious pizza crust and, once you've tried it, you may never order out again. It's a little bit more trouble, but it's worth it! It can be topped with sliced tomatoes, fontina, goat cheese and peppers. Be creative!

- 2 t or ½ package of yeast
- 3 c all-purpose flour
- 1 t sugar
- 1 t salt
- 2 T olive oil
- 1 c water
- 1 c sourdough starter (see p. 74)

Select "dough" mode on your bread machine.

Add ingredients in the order listed and push "Start."

This makes two 9″ pizzas. Freeze them, or top and bake at 475 degrees for 12–15 minutes, or until cheese is melted and bubbly and the crust is lightly browned.

Note: This dough only needs one rise.

Regency Rolls

These are scrumptious tender dinner rolls best enhanced by sweet creamery butter. An excellent roll with Thanksgiving dinner!

BATTER:

- 2 t or 1/2 package of yeast
- 3 c bread flour
- 1 1/2 t salt
- 1 1/2 T sugar
- 2 T nonfat dry milk
- 4 1/2 T butter
- 1 c + 2 t water
- 1 large egg

GLAZE:

- 1 egg, beaten with
- 1 T water

Select "dough" mode on your bread machine.

Add the ingredients in the order listed and push "Start."

When the dough is finished, divide it into 12 equal balls. Put the balls on a lightly greased cookie pan and let them rise, in a draft-free area, for 30 minutes.

With your hands, roll the balls into egg shapes. Using a roller, roll them out to 1/8″ thick. Roll the strips starting at the thin end to form crescents.

Return the rolls to the pan and let rise 50 minutes. Preheat the oven to 375 degrees.

Brush the rolls with the beaten egg and water glaze and bake for 15–18 minutes, or until golden brown.

Croissants

Croissants are tricky to make, but it doesn't take long to learn and it's really worth it! Store-bought croissants don't compare, and bakery croissants are often terribly expensive. Put these out for Sunday breakfast with butter, cinnamon, and jams.

3 t or 1 package of yeast
3 c bread flour
2 T + 2 t sugar
1½ t salt
1 T + 2 t butter
1 egg
1¼ c water
¾ c (1½ sticks) chilled butter

Put all the ingredients except for egg and butter into the bread machine and select "dough" or "manual" setting.

At the end of the cycle, remove the dough and spread it evenly across the bottom of a large baking dish or cookie sheet and freeze it for one hour.

Remove the dough from the freezer and roll it out to about ¼" thick. Slice the butter into 1 teaspoon pats and cover the flattened dough with them. Fold the dough in thirds and roll it out again to ¼" thickness. Repeat two more times, rolling after each fold.

Cover the dough and put it in the refrigerator for one hour. Then remove it, fold it and roll it three times, and return it to the freezer for one hour.

Remove the dough from the freezer and roll it out to a rectangle ⅛" thick and brush it lightly with the beaten egg. Cut the dough into triangles, and roll them up from the wide end. Bend them into a crescent shape.

Cover the croissants and leave them to rise for one hour, or until they have doubled in size. Brush them with the remaining beaten egg and bake at 375 degrees for 10 minutes, or until golden brown.

Brioche

In college I took a vacation in Paris with some friends who treated me first class all the way. Every morning at the Hotel dê Notre Dame in the Latin Quarter, we would have cool brioche spread with cold butter and jam and served with rich coffee.

- 2 t or ½ package of yeast
- 3 c bread flour
- 3 T plus 1 t sugar
- 2 t salt
- 3 eggs
- 4 T butter
- 1 c milk

Set your bread machine on the "dough" or "manual" setting and let it do the hard work for you. Add all ingredients except one egg and one teaspoon of sugar.

When the dough is ready, remove it from the machine and divide it into 12 equal balls. Take a small amount of dough from each ball and make another, smaller ball.

Grease a muffin tin and put one large ball in each cup. Press a valley into the center of each large ball and put a small ball into the depression.

Cover with a dish cloth and let rise for 45 minutes.

Preheat oven to 375 degrees.

Lightly beat the reserved egg with the one teaspoon of sugar and brush a bit of the mixture onto each brioche. Put into the preheated oven and bake for 15–20 minutes, or until lightly browned.

Hamburger Buns and Hot Dog Rolls

These hamburger buns and hot dog rolls are so easy to make that you need never rush to the grocery store at the last minute for a summer cookout again. And your friends will be amazed at how good your homemade rolls are when compared with the standard fare.

- 2 t or ½ package of yeast
- 3 c bread flour
- 2 T sugar
- 2 t salt
- 3 T nonfat dry milk powder
- 2 T butter
- 1 c water
- poppy or sesame seeds (optional)

Set your bread machine to "dough" or "manual" setting. Add all ingredients, except poppy/sesame seeds, and push "Start." Let it knead and rest your dough.

When the dough is ready, remove it from the machine and divide it into twelve equal parts. Shape each part into the appropriate shape (long and slender for hot dogs, round and flat-ish for hamburger buns).

Cover the rolls and let them rise in a warm, draft-free place for 1 hour.

Heat the oven to 375 degrees.

Sprinkle poppy seeds or sesame seeds on top of the rolls (if you like) and bake them for 20 minutes or until they are browned. Slice them open with a fork.

Onion Sandwich Rolls

You may want to serve these savory rolls as dinner rolls with stews and beef dishes. Actually, the onions are optional.

- 2 t or ½ package of yeast
- 3 c bread flour
- 2 t sugar
- 2 t salt
- ¼ c minced onion
- 2 T light vegetable oil
- 1 c buttermilk

Set your bread machine to "dough" or "manual" setting, add all ingredients, and let the machine do the hard work for you.

When the dough is ready, remove it from the machine and divide it into 12 equal balls.

Cover the balls and let them rise in a warm, draft-free place for 1 hour.

Heat the oven to 375 degrees. Cook the rolls on a lightly greased cookie sheet for 20 minutes, or until they are lightly browned.

Whole Wheat Rolls

This is another sandwich roll or hamburger/hot dog bun to try. The whole wheat makes it a little more nutritious and many people prefer the heartier flavor.

2 t or ½ package of yeast	1 T honey
1½ c bread flour	2 t salt
1 c whole wheat flour	2 T light vegetable oil
¼ c wheat germ	1¼ c water
¼ c nonfat dry milk powder	

Set your bread machine to "dough" or "manual" setting, add all ingredients, and let the machine do the hard work for you.

When the dough is ready, remove it from the machine and divide it into 12 equal balls.

Cover the balls and let them rise in a warm, draft-free place for 1 hour.

Heat the oven to 375 degrees. Cook the rolls on a lightly greased cookie sheet for 20 minutes, or until they are lightly browned.

Challah

When I began making bread by hand, someone asked me if I had a recipe for Challah. Unbelievably, I had never heard of it. I looked it up in Beard on Bread *and sent it to my friend. Then I began to experiment with it myself. This bread is delicious, of course, but it's also very pretty and it makes a terrific addition to a brunch buffet.*

2 t or ½ package of yeast	3 T butter
3 c bread flour	2 eggs
2 T sugar	1 c water
2 t salt	poppy seeds (optional)

Set your machine to "dough" or "manual" setting, and add all ingredients except the poppy seeds. Push "Start" and let the machine do the work for you.

When the dough is ready, remove it from the machine and divide it into 3 equal parts. Put them on a cookie sheet and join them all at the very top. Then, very carefully, braid them down to the bottom.

Cover the braid with a dishcloth and let it rise in a warm, draft-free place for 45 minutes.

Lightly beat an egg with 1 t sugar and brush the mixture over the braid. Before it dries, sprinkle it with poppy seeds.

Bake at 375 degrees for 45 minutes, or until the top is lightly browned.

Pita Bread*

Pita is good for almost everything. I served hamburgers in pita to a finicky friend and was shocked at how much he loved them. I like to slip some sharp cheddar into a pita pocket and toast it and eat it with fresh tomato soup.

- 2 t or ½ package of yeast
- 1½ c bread flour
- 1 c whole wheat flour
- 1 T sugar
- 1 t salt
- 2 T olive oil
- 1 c water

Set your machine to "dough" or "manual". Add all ingredients and push "Start."

When the dough is ready, remove it from the machine and divide it into 8 equal balls. Put them on a cookie sheet and cover with a dishcloth. Let rise for 30 minutes.

Heat the oven to broil or 550 degrees.

Roll each ball out to a very flat disk. Place them back on the cookie sheet and cook them very quickly in the hot oven—about 4 minutes per side is all that's required.

* This recipe is dairy-free.

Fresh Bread Sticks

Serve these bread sticks with a spaghetti dinner. You can also add one-half cup grated parmesan cheese to the dough recipe, and serve the bread sticks with pizza sauce as dip.

- 2 t or ½ package of yeast
- 3 c bread flour
- 1 T sugar
- 1 t salt
- 1 T butter
- 1 c milk
- 1 egg white mixed with 1 t water, set aside

Select the "dough" or "manual" mode on your bread machine. Add ingredients, except egg white/water mixture, in the order listed and push "Start."

When the dough is ready, remove it from the bread machine and divide it into 12 equal pieces on a cookie sheet. Cover and let rise in a warm, draft-free spot for 20 minutes.

Roll each piece into a long strip and brush it with the egg white mixture. Sprinkle lightly with garlic salt, if desired. Bake at 400 degrees for about 15 minutes. When they are lightly browned they will be chewy. If you want them crisp, lower the heat to 300 degrees after the first 15 minutes, then check them every 5 minutes for doneness.

Pretzels*

Everyone has a ton of mustards in their refrigerators; take them all out and have a sampling party, dipping these pretzels in and eating them.

2 t or ½ package of yeast
3 c unbleached white flour
1 T sugar
½ t salt
2 T margarine (or butter)
1 c water
1 quart water
5 t baking soda
coarse salt (either kosher or sea)

Put the yeast, flour, sugar, ½ teaspoon of salt, butter and 1 cup of water into your bread machine on the "dough" or "manual" setting.

When the dough is ready, remove it and divide it into 12 equal parts (or more, if you want your pretzels smaller). Roll them into long strands and shape them into pretzels.

Set the pretzels on a cookie sheet and cover with a dish cloth. Let them rise in a warm, draft-free place for 45 minutes.

Put 1 quart of water and 5 teaspoons of baking soda in a large nonaluminum saucepan, and bring it to the simmering stage just before boiling. Reduce heat to low before the water gets a chance to boil.

Carefully drop the pretzels into the hot water for 1 minute each. Remove them with a slotted spoon and put them on a greased cookie sheet.

When they are all boiled and removed to the cookie sheet, sprinkle the pretzels with a small amount of coarse salt (kosher or sea salt).

Bake at 475 degrees for 10–12 minutes, or until browned.

* This recipe is dairy-free.

Bagels*

You can be pretty creative with bagels. I like to add one-quarter cup of chopped onion to my recipe, but you could also add raisins, cinnamon, or whatever you like best.

3 t or 1 package of yeast
3 c unbleached white flour
2 T sugar
2 t salt
1 c water
1 quart water

Put all the ingredients into your bread machine and set it to "dough" or "manual".

Let it knead and rise once, then remove the dough and turn the machine off—you don't want bagels to become too airy.

Divide the dough into 12 equal pieces and roll them each into a thick cord and form it into a circle (wetting the ends to make it stick together). You may also leave each piece in a ball and punch your thumbs through, forming the circle that way.

Grease a cookie sheet and put the bagels on it. Cover them with a dish cloth and let them rise in a warm, draft-free place for 15 minutes.

Bring 1 quart of water to a hard boil in a large, nonaluminum pot. Drop the bagels in, a couple at a time, and let them boil for about 30 seconds, or until they rise to the top. Remove them with a slotted spoon and drain them well on paper towels.

Heat the oven to 550 degrees.

Return the bagels to the greased cookie sheet and put them in the oven for 8–10 minutes, or until they are lightly browned.

* This recipe is dairy-free.

Recipes for Allergy Sufferers

If you suffer from food allergies, or know someone who does, you can still make good bread that won't leave you aching, sniffling, or otherwise miserable. Here are several recipes for wheat-free breads. Also, at the end of this book, you'll find a listing of ingredients to use as substitutes for milk, eggs, and wheat.

Wheat-Free White Bread

Experiment with this bread and learn to make whatever variations you like: if you can eat eggs, add one for a wheat-free Sally Lunn bread. Try adding one-half cup grated parmesan cheese and herbs. Experiment and see what works for you.

- 2 t or ½ package of yeast
- 2½ c potato flour
- 2 t sugar
- 1 t salt
- ½ c milk, scalded
- ½ c water

Add all the ingredients to the machine in the order listed. Choose either regular or light crust (depending on your preference) and push "Start."

Wheat-Free Cheese Bread

For visible lumps of cheese, cut one whole bar of cheddar into large-ish lumps and add them at the end of the second kneading (or at the indicator beep, if you have one).

- 2 t or ½ package of yeast
- 2½ c potato flour
- 2 t sugar
- 1 t salt
- ¼ c shredded sharp cheddar cheese
- ½ c scalded milk
- ½ c water

Add all the ingredients to the machine in the order listed. Choose either regular or light crust (depending on your preference) and push "Start."

Wheat-Free Rye Bread*

The rye flour from the grocery store is medium rye, which works well for this recipe. If you prefer, though, you may use dark or light rye from the health food store.

2 t or ½ package of yeast	2 t baking powder
½ c potato flour	1 t margarine (or butter)
1½ c rye flour	⅞ c milk or water
½ t salt	

Add all the ingredients to the machine in the order listed. Choose either regular or light crust (depending on your preference) and push "Start."

* This recipe is dairy-free.

Wheat-Free Oatmeal Bread*

Keep an eye on the consistency of this dough in the early stages of kneading. If necessary, add 1 tablespoon of water at a time until you have a firm but soft dough.

2 t or ½ package of yeast	¼ c honey
2 c potato flour	1 t salt
½ c rolled oats, old-fashioned or quick	2 t margarine (or butter)
	1 c water

Add all the ingredients to the machine in the order listed. Choose either regular or light crust (depending on your preference) and push "Start."

* This recipe is dairy-free.

Wheat-Free Sweet Potato Bread*

Use your leftover Thanksgiving sweet potatoes for this recipe or make it ahead of time while you're cooking.

- 2 t or 1/2 package of yeast
- 1/2 c rolled oats
- 1/4 c potato flour
- 1/2 c mashed sweet potatoes
- 2 t baking powder
- 1 T honey
- 1/2 t salt
- 2 T margarine (or butter)
- 1/4 c chopped walnuts
- 1/4 c raisins
- 2/3 c water

Add all the ingredients to the machine in the order listed. Choose either regular or light crust (depending on your preference) and push "Start."

* This recipe is dairy-free.

Spreads 'n Stuff

Now that you have all this fabulous bread, what are you going to do with it? Well, if it makes it from the machine to the table without being eaten, you're in luck! Just in case, here are some ideas for spreads and sandwiches and other things to do with bread.

Welsh Rarebit

This is a good thing to serve over sandwich-type breads, such as any of the whites or whole grains. However, if you want it extra cheesy, you may serve it over cheddar cheese bread.

¼ c butter
¼ c flour
½ t salt
½ t dry mustard
½ t Worcestershire sauce
¾ c milk
1 can (12 oz) flat beer
2 c shredded cheddar cheese
8 slices toast

Melt the butter in 2-quart saucepan over low heat.

Add the flour, salt, mustard, and Worcestershire sauce, stirring constantly until the mixture is smooth and bubbly. Remove it from the heat. Stir in the milk and pour in the beer and return it to the burner. Heat to boiling, stirring constantly. Add cheese and keep over heat, stirring frequently, until the cheese has completely melted.

Arrange the toast slices on ungreased cookie sheet. Spoon about ⅓ c sauce onto each slice. Set oven control to broil or 550 degrees. Broil until cheese is very bubbly and lightly browned (about three minutes).

Raspberry Jam*

You may make this jam from raspberries, strawberries, blueberries, and blackberries, all of which I have tried successfully. You may also use two pounds of frozen (but thawed) berries, but the flavor is not always as fresh.

2 lbs fresh raspberries, cleaned
4 t lemon juice
2 lbs very fine sugar

Put the berries and lemon juice into a large pot. Heat slowly over low heat, mashing the berries with a spoon or the bottom of a glass, until the mixture boils. Simmer, stirring constantly, for five minutes.

Spread the sugar in a metal baking pan and heat it in the oven for five minutes at about 350 degrees.

Add the warmed sugar to the simmering berries and stir them all over low heat until the sugar is dissolved (about 15 minutes). Turn the heat up and boil hard for five minutes, stirring often.

Test the jam for readiness by dropping a bit on a chilled plate. Return the plate to the freezer for two minutes. Take it out and inspect it; if the jam has thickened and formed a skin, it's ready to be jarred and stored.

* This recipe is dairy-free.

Sugar-Free Strawberry Jam*

Make this jam in small amounts because it can only be stored in the refrigerator for about a week.

Fresh berries are always terrific, but you may use frozen ones as well.

2 pints of strawberries, hulled (if frozen, thaw first)
3/4 c frozen apple juice concentrate

Put about half of the berries into a large saucepan. Puree the other half in a blender or food processor and add them to the saucepan and turn the heat on to medium.

Simmer the berries for about 15–20 minutes, or until they are cooked.

Mix in the apple juice concentrate and turn the heat to medium-high. Boil hard for 15 minutes, then test the jam for readiness by dropping a bit on a chilled plate. Return the plate to the freezer for two minutes. Take it out and inspect it; if the jam has thickened and formed a skin, it's ready to be jarred and stored.

* This recipe is dairy-free.

Apple Butter*

Apple butter is a favorite for young and old alike. Because it's sweet, it makes an excellent accompaniment to any sweet bread. Cinnamon Raisin Bread and Apple Butter would make a wonderful autumn gift.

- 3½ lbs tart green apples
- 2 c apple cider
- 1 c sugar
- 1 c brown sugar
- ½ t allspice
- ¾ t cinnamon
- ½ t nutmeg
- ¼ t ground cloves
- ⅛ t salt
- 2 T molasses

Quarter, peel and core the apples. Cook the peels and cores in the cider, covered, for about ½ hour. Strain the cider and discard the solids. Add the apples and all remaining ingredients to the cider and simmer the mixture, stirring often, until the apples are very soft. Puree.

Resume cooking the apple butter on low until it is very thick and smooth. Cool before storing.

* This recipe is dairy-free.

French Toast Toppings

There are a million things you can drizzle over French toast. The most common toppings are maple syrup and powdered sugar (my own favorite). Here are two more toppings to try.

Butter Syrup

1 c maple syrup
¼ c (½ stick) butter
¼ c water
½ t vanilla extract (or almond extract)

Heat the maple syrup and water in a small saucepan over low to medium heat. When it begins a slow boil, add the butter and stir until it's melted. Add the extract, stir well, and serve.

Jam Syrup

I imagine this would work with any jelly or preserves that you have; I have tried it with berry preserves and grape jelly.

1 c preserves or jelly
½ c (1 stick) butter
½ c water

Heat the preserves and water in a small saucepan over medium heat until the mixture begins a slow boil. Be careful not to turn the heat up too high, as the preserves burn very quickly.

When the mixture is boiling, add the butter and stir constantly until the butter is melted and well blended. Serve hot.

Breakfast Spreads

I like to make these spreads and put each in a fancy little china bowl and set them out with Sunday breakfast or brunch. But don't limit them to breakfast only: Have them at tea or with small slices of bread set out at a cocktail party. Another nice idea is to get some small plastic containers and include one or two spreads with a loaf of bread as a gift.

Whipped Butter

½ c (1 stick) butter, room temperature.
¼ c whipping cream

Put both ingredients into a small mixing bowl and whip at high spead to a smooth, creamy consistency. Serve.

Cinnamon Butter

½ c (1 stick) butter, room temperature
¼ c whipping cream
¼ c cinnamon sugar

Whip the butter and cream together to a smooth consistency then stir the cinnamon sugar in gently with a wooden spoon for a marbled effect. Serve.

Raspberry Butter

¼ c (½ stick) butter, room temperature

2 T whipping cream or milk

½ c raspberry (or other) preserves

Whip the butter and whipping cream together, then stir the preserves in gently with a wooden spoon. For a smoother raspberry butter, whip all of the ingredients together. Serve.

Berry Cream Cheese

8 oz (1 package) cream cheese

2 T whipping cream or milk

½ c preserves

Beat the cream cheese and whipping cream together to a smooth consistency then stir the preserves in. Serve.

Orange Cream Cheese

8 oz (1 package) of cream cheese

½ c orange juice

2 t orange rind

Beat all ingredients together in a small mixing bowl. You may garnish with a little bit of extra orange rind sprinkled on top. Serve.

Peanut Butter Cream Cheese Spread

4 oz (1/2 package) of cream cheese
3/4 c peanut butter (chunky or smooth)
1 t sugar

Combine all ingredients in a small mixing bowl and beat at high speed with a hand mixer. Serve.

Tofu Peanut Butter and Banana Spread

12 oz tofu (1 package), drained	2 small, ripe bananas
1/2 c peanut butter	2 T honey
	1 T lemon juice

Puree all ingredients in a blender or food processor. You may top this spread with crushed nuts or raisins, then serve.

Yogurt Cream Cheese

Line a colander or strainer with white paper towels or cheese cloth. Put 1 container of plain yogurt in, cover the top with plastic wrap, and allow it to drain for 24 hours at room temperature. Chill, then serve.

Tofu Cream Cheese

12 oz (1 package) soft tofu, drained and squeezed between two plates to make sure there is no moisture left	2 T light vegetable oil
	1 t lemon juice
	1/2 t salt
	dash pepper

Puree all ingredients in a blender or food processor until smooth and thick. Chill and serve.

Sandwich Spreads

These are heartier spreads for making open-faced or regular sandwiches.

Tofu Egg Spread

- 12 oz (1 package) soft tofu, drained and squeezed between two plates to make sure there is no moisture left
- 2 hard-boiled eggs, diced
- 2 T light vegetable oil
- 2 T lemon juice
- ½ t salt
- 2 T finely minced onion
- 1 T dried chopped parsley

Combine all ingredients in a blender or food processor and puree to a smooth, thick consistency. Serve.

Cream Cheese Veggie Spread

- 8 oz (1 package) cream cheese
- 1 carrot, finely diced
- 1 red pepper, finely diced
- 1 radish, finely diced
- 1 small onion, finely diced

Beat the cream cheese to smooth with a hand mixer. Stir the diced vegetables in by hand. Serve.

Olive Spread

1 c olives, pitted (pimentos are okay)
8 oz (1 package) cream cheese
2 T whipping cream or milk

Combine all ingredients in a blender or food processor and puree to a smooth, thick consistency. Serve.

Walnut Olive Spread

8 oz (1 package) cream cheese
½ c chopped walnuts
½ c chopped olives
¼ c chopped scallions

Spread the walnuts on a cookie sheet and toast them in a 350 degree oven for 10–15 minutes.

Stir all the ingredients together in a small bowl and serve.

Cottage Cheese Nut and Herb Spread

1 c cottage cheese (or 1 package of cream cheese)
2 T dill weed
½ c chopped walnuts
¼ c chopped dates, optional

Combine all ingredients and chill. You may garnish your sandwich with watercress or cilantro. Serve.

Hummus

2 c cooked or canned chick peas (garbanzo beans)
½–¾ c chick pea liquid (either the cooking water or canned)
3 T lemon juice
½ c tahini (sesame paste)
2–3 cloves garlic, minced
1 t salt
dash cayenne, for garnish
fresh parsley, for garnish

Puree all of the ingredients together to make a smooth, thick consistency. Garnish with cayenne and parsley and use as a sandwich filling or as a dip for warm slices of pita.

Basil Pesto

This is an absolutely heavenly spread. I like it better on bread than pasta, particularly bread painted with olive oil, then grilled with thin slices of onion and grated romano cheese.

This recipe calls for a lot of garlic, but even people who don't think they like garlic love this spread.

Taste as you go along—you may prefer more salt or cheese or even garlic. Use more olive oil if you need to smooth the consistency.

- 1/4 c olive oil
- 1 c basil leaves
- 7 cloves garlic, minced
- 1/4 c pine nuts or walnuts
- 1/2 c pecorino Romano cheese, grated
- 1 T butter

Toast the pine nuts or walnuts for ten minutes at 350 degrees. Be careful when you take them out; they're very hot.

Combine all the ingredients in a blender or food processor and whir to a smooth consistency.

Chill pesto, then serve.

Six Things To Do With Leftover Bread

1. Feed the ducks!

2. Make croutons: cut the bread into small cubes, heat some olive oil (about 1 tablespoonful) and garlic (2 minced cloves) in a skillet, and brown the bread cubes to crisp. Serve them in salads and on soups, particularly gazpacho!

3. Make fondue bread: cut the bread into cubes and spread them on a cookie sheet. Bake at 250 degrees for 15 minutes to make them crisp but not cooked.

4. Make breading for meat, fish or poultry filets. Toast the bread to make sure it's very crisp. Put it in the food processor or blender, or even in a bag which you can beat on the outside, and make very fine crumbs. You may add herbs, such as Italian Seasoning.

For chicken filets: dip chicken breasts in lightly beaten egg or melted butter, then in bread crumbs. Drizzle lemon juice on top and bake at 350 degrees until done (usually ½ hour for average-sized chicken breasts).

5. Make bread pudding: In a large mixing bowl, cream together 1 cup sugar, ½ cup soft butter, 3 eggs, 1½ cups milk, ½ can (6 oz) evaporated milk, 1 tablespoon nutmeg, and 1 tablespoon vanilla. Add one-half to one loaf's worth of bread cubes. Pour everything into a greased casserole dish and bake 1 hour at 350 degrees, stir it, turn the oven up to 375 degrees and bake 1 more hour, until the top is lightly browned.

6. Make stuffing: This varies, depending on the size of the bird you need to stuff, or the amount of bread you've got leftover. For one loaf: heat 1½ cups of water in a saucepan with 1 stick of butter. When the butter has melted add two stalks of chopped celery, one large chopped onion, one tablespoon of sage, one tablespoon of poultry seasoning, and salt and pepper to taste. Stir in the bread and add water, if desired, to make the stuffing more moist.

Appendix

Trouble-Shooting

IF THE MACHINE DOES NOT OPERATE . . .

- Is it plugged in?
- Is the pan in securely?
- Did the electricity go off and reset the machine?
- Is the inside still too hot from the last loaf?

IF SMOKE IS COMING FROM THE VENT . . .

- Ingredients (wet or dry) may have spilled over onto the heating element and will burn off.
- If the smoke is *not* coming from spilled ingredients, unplug the machine and call the manufacturer for further assistance.

IF THE BREAD IS COLLAPSED AND THE BOTTOM IS DAMP . . .

- You probably left the bread in the pan for too long; try to remove it within ½ hour of baking completion unless your machine has a cooling fan.

IF THE BREAD RISES TOO MUCH . . .

- Did you add too much flour?
- Did you add too much yeast?
- If the dough is still in the rising stage when you notice it's over-risen, you may tear a handful of it off and let the machine continue.

IF THE BREAD DOESN'T RISE ENOUGH . . .

- Did you remember to add the yeast?
- Did you add enough liquid? (Or did the dough thump heavily during kneading? If so, add liquid 1 T at a time.)
- Did you remember to add the sugar or honey (or other natural sweetener)?
- Was the flour very old?
- Was the yeast old or expired?

IF THE TOP OF THE BREAD HAS DRY FLOUR ON IT . . .

- The kneading blade is probably not secure.

IF THE BREAD IS UNDERCOOKED AND/OR STICKY . . .

- Was there a power failure during baking? (Check the digital clocks in the rest of the house.)
- Did someone accidentally hit the stop button during operation?
- Was the top opened during baking?
- Was the machine properly set, or was it set for "Dough"?

IF THE TOP AND SIDES ARE BROWNED BUT THE CENTER IS STICKY . . .

- Did you use enough flour?
- Did you use too much liquid?

For Further Reading

Beard, James. **Beard on Bread**, Ballantine Books, New York. *This is an excellent source of information on all aspects of breadmaking.*

Elliot, Rose. **The Complete Vegetarian Cuisine**, Pantheon Books, New York. *This is my favorite cookbook; it has excellent suggestions for sandwiches, including pita sandwiches and things to pack for children's lunches. I have all of this author's books, and I recommend them highly.*

Katzen, Mollie. **The Moosewood Cookbook**, **The Enchanted Broccoli Forest**, and **Still Life with Menu** all published by Ten Speed Press, Berkeley, CA. *All of these books contain great sandwich ideas.*

Klavan, Ellen. **The Creative Lunchbox**, Crown Publishers, New York. *As a mother, I find this little book indispensable. There are tons of ideas here for sandwiches and other treats for finicky kids (of all ages).*

Robertson, Laurel, et al. **Laurel's Kitchen**, Ten Speed Press, Berkeley, CA. *This is an unbeatable source book, full of information on nutrition and ingredients and terrific healthful recipes.*

Ingredient Substitutions

The following lists are adapted from *Recipes for Allergies*, a wonderful cookbook by Billie Little (Grosset and Dunlap, 1969).

MILK: 1 C =

1 c water + 3 T nondairy creamer powder
3/4 c nondairy creamer + 1/4 c water
1 c soy milk

BUTTER:

margarine
soy margarine
olive oil
light vegetable oil

GRAINS: 1 C =

1 c corn flour
1 c rye flour
1 c potato flour
1 c rice flour
3/4 c buckwheat
1 1/3 c rolled oats
1/2 c rye flour + 1/2 c potato flour
1/3 c potato flour + 2/3 c rye flour
1/2 c potato flour + 1/2 c soy flour
5/8 c rice flour + 1/3 c rye flour

Consistencies vary greatly and your dough may be much thinner than ordinary wheat dough. There is a world of possibilities; just experiment.

INDEX